THE
POPULATION
OF
HEAVEN

THE
POPULATION
O F
HEAVEN

DR. RAMESH RICHARD

MOODY PRESS
CHICAGO

© 1994 by
RAMESH RICHARD

All Scripture quotations, unless indicated, are taken from the *New American Standard Bible,* © 1960, 1962, 1963, 1968, 1971, 1972, 1973, 1975, and 1977 by The Lockman Foundation, and are used by permission.

Scripture quotations marked (NIV) are taken from the *Holy Bible: New International Version®.* NIV®. Copyright © 1973, 1978, 1984 International Bible Society. Used by permission of Zondervan Publishing House. All rights reserved.

ISBN: 0-8024-3946-2

1 3 5 7 9 10 8 6 4 2

Printed in the United States of America

To my father-in-law,
Pastor Jack M. Perry,
who pays close attention to life and doctrine

1 Timothy 4:16

CONTENTS

Acknowledgments

Special thanks go to my wife, Bonnie, and to my children, Ryan, Robby, and Sitara, who prayed daily for "Daddy's book"; to Dallas Seminary, RREACH International, and to the Grytes, who provided the time and resources for me to use a sabbatical effectively.

INTRODUCTION

Explosive growth in global population rates forces a most energetic question on all evangelicals, "Are the masses of the world condemned to endless conscious punishment, even though they cannot be faulted for not having heard the gospel of Christ during their earthly life?" Most evangelicals insist on an exclusivist position. They maintain that explicit knowledge of the Lord Jesus Christ followed by faith in Him alone are necessary for eternal salvation. They also are aware that vast numbers of mankind are prohibited by history, geography, religion, culture, and Christian failure from having access to an explicit presentation of Christ's salvation.[1] Consequently, evangelical exclusivism grimaces under emotional trauma and theological uneasiness.

EXCLUSIVISM CREATES EMOTIONAL PAIN

The emotional pain that results from an affirmative answer to the sobering question just posed cannot be masked. The sheer vastness of the growing number of the unevangelized overwhelms the crustiest of Christian hearts. If I could elevate sentiment to the status of truth, the ghastly biblical doctrine of hell would be the first one to be revised or rejected. Emotional pain for exclusivists is imperative. Inasmuch as Jesus cried over Jerusalem's rejection of God's salvation (Matt. 23:37), our tear ducts need not remain dry knowing that masses are unexposed to the gospel. Just as Paul was consumed by Israel's need for salvation (Rom. 10:1) and aspired to preach the gospel where Christ was not named (Rom. 15:20), our sound sleep patterns need not be undisturbed over eternal damnation. Because God states His desire for all men to repent (2 Peter 3:9), an uneasy anxiety for the lost must be evident in our lifestyle. If people who are not given the opportunity to repent are also really condemned to endless conscious punishment, then weeping, insomnia, and anxiety are appropriate to the question. The emotional anguish is unbearable.

EXCLUSIVISM GENERATES INTELLECTUAL TENSION

Further, the intellectual stress in the theological question refuses to go away. The basic intellectual challenge facing evangelical exclusivity is not only hoisted by prideful intellectuals on university campuses, but also by thoughtful Christians all over the globe. "What about the 'heathen' in India or Africa?"; "What about our ancestors who did not hear the gospel?"; "What about positive features in non-Christian religions which have sustained cultures for millennia?"; and so forth. First-generation converts to the Christian faith often mix the emotional and intellectual levels of questioning as they sorrow over the death of a moral, sincere, and loving non-Christian relative. The combination of the intellectual tensions and emotional realities implied in the traditional evangelical position on salvation complicates the question enormously.

There is no other contemporary topic that calls for the integration of theological, biblical, and missiological thinking as does the nettlesome issue of the number and destiny of the unevangelized. As thorny as that issue is for evangelicals, it is a consequent of a parent doctrine of "a theology of religions" and a grandparent doctrine of "the uniqueness of Jesus Christ." Together, "this cluster of issues energizes a whole range of theological topics and makes practically everything come alive with fresh relevance and power."[2]

INCLUSIVISM INCREASES THE POPULATION OF HEAVEN

Disputing exclusivism is inclusivism, a soteriological (salvation) hypothesis gaining momentum within evangelicalism. It contests the soteriology of exclusive evangelicalism as being demanded by Scripture and as being emotionally satisfactory. Instead, an inclusivist theology of salvation contends that explicit knowledge of Christ in this lifetime is not necessary for eternal salvation. It asserts that universal accessibility of salvation is possible without the hearing of the Christian gospel. This theological stance hopes to depopulate hell and make heaven more crowded than the eternal scenarios of exclusivist evangelicalism.

Inclusivism is engagingly and best propounded by an influential Canadian theologian, Clark H. Pinnock.[3] Well-known among North American evangelicals for fine defenses of the Christian faith and biblical inerrancy in his early theological writings,[4] his sensitivity and creativity have moved him away from a distinctly evangelical stance of a high view of Scripture[5] as well as from the traditional position concerning the destiny of the unevangelized.[6]

A CRITIQUE OF INCLUSIVISM

The primary purpose of this book is to appraise inclusivism from an exclusivist platform. Biblical material and theological argument pertaining to the unevangelized's fate is communicated as a supplement to the appraisal.[7] A critical searchlight is shined on soteriological inclusivism regarding its premises, arguments, exegesis, and conclusions. Even though this work is not intended to be a straightforward exposition of exegetical evidence and doctrinal propositions on the subject,[8] a profile of an exclusivist, evangelical Christology, an evangelical theology of religions, and a scriptural view of the destiny of the unevangelized will emerge in the main sections and notes.

We shall heed the following format in this evaluation and exposition. Chapter 1 constitutes a brief overview of inclusivist arguments, along with a quick critique of professed motivations in the proposal. Chapters 2 and 3 scrutinize the biblical and theological foundations of the inclusivist position. Chapter 4 contains an extended evaluation of an inclusivist theology of religions. Chapter 5 suggests directions and resources for answering the critical question from an evangelical theology of discontinuity.

I hope this labor will participate in the evangelical community's responsibility to construct a consistent theology of religions in the face of increasing pluralism; a comprehensive theology of missions in the face of diminishing motivation; and an authentic definition of the term *evangelical* in the face of broadening redefinition. I did not interact with the inclusivist position as long as it dominated the agenda of liberal Protestant and Roman Catholic writers.[9] Pinnock and Sanders, however, relate to evangelicals and find a problem with the traditional view being termed evangelical at all. Pinnock asks, "What does 'evangelical' mean when applied to those who want to ensure that there is as little Good News as possible?" (WGM, 163). He remarks: "It is a little ironical that the term *evangelical* would come to refer to a theology that in certain expressions looks more like an attack on the Good News of the New Testament" (WGM, 41; italics in the original). Throughout this book one will observe that the term (and a theology of) "good news" (*euaggelion*) refers not only to effect, i.e.,"good" (*eu*); but to epistemology (knowledge of), i.e., "news" (*aggelion*).

I also desire that this longer response will create theological restlessness for those who may consider inclusivist theses as viable within evangelicalism. With the emergence of the issue on the forefront of biblical, theological, philosophical, and missiological debate, the question is not how evangelicalism will thrive, but whether it will survive the articulate intellectual friction that inclusivism generates at different levels. The identity of the evangelical community, the intelligibility of the biblical faith, and the applicability of Christian truth are all at stake.[10] How evangelicals negotiate the restrictive exclusivity, ontological uniqueness, absolute finality, comprehensive sufficiency, and epistemological necessity of the only God and Savior, the Lord Jesus Christ, will not only determine evangelical destiny but the destiny of the unevangelized. The latter's destiny, after all, is the critical question.

Notes

1. Different solutions to this tension have been proposed from evangelical platforms throughout history. John Sanders's *No Other Name: An Investigation into the Destiny of the Unevangelized* (Grand Rapids: Eerdmans, 1992) delineates the following views with reliable historical documentation: restrictivism (all the unevangelized are damned), universalism (all the unevangelized are saved), a wider hope universal evangelization before death, a wider hope post-mortem evangelization, and inclusivism (universally accessible salvation apart from evangelization). Even though universalism has not been an evangelical option, less favored and recognized positions such as post-mortem evangelization and inclusivism have been defended by evangelicals in the past.

2. Clark H. Pinnock, *A Wideness in God's Mercy: The Finality of Jesus Christ in a World of Religions* (Grand Rapids: Zondervan, 1992), 183. The book shall be cited as *WGM* in the rest of this work.

3. We include John Sanders's book (see n. 1 above; *NON* hence) in this critical examination as well. Sanders conveys the convergence of theological issues around this topic too:

   More significant is the particular stance one takes regarding christology, faith, the nature and means of grace, the value of general revelation, the ministry of the Holy Spirit, and epistemology. The question of the unevangelized intersects with such vital issues as the nature of God (his love and power), the problem of evil, and election and damnation. (*NON*, 31)

   There are intense connections between Pinnock's and Sanders's books. Pinnock reverentially endorses Sanders's work; and Sanders cites Pinnock more than any other contemporary figure in the broad evangelical spectrum.

4. See his *Set Forth Your Case: An Examination of Christianity's Credentials* (Chicago: Moody, 1967); and *Biblical Revelation: The Foundation of Christian Theology* (Chicago: Moody, 1971).

5. A quick reading of his *Tracking the Maze* (New York: Harper & Row, 1990) alerts evangelicals to this theological movement. See also Robert M. Price, "Clark H. Pinnock: Conservative and Contemporary," *Evangelical Quarterly* 88:2 (1988): 157–83 and Robert V. Rakestraw, "Clark H. Pinnock: A Theological Odyssey," *Christian Scholar's Review* 19 (March 1990): 252–70. This vacillation (Pinnock's self-description, ibid., 267, n. 77) could also be documented by the theological persuasion of the schools in which he has occupied professorial positions. He presently teaches at the McMaster Divinity College, Hamilton, Ontario, Canada. Early teaching stints included the Trinity Evangelical Divinity School in Chicago, Illinois, and Regent College, Vancouver, British Columbia, Canada. Pinnock has also endorsed a biography of his shifts in Ray C. W. Roenfeldt, *Clark H. Pinnock on Biblical Authority: An Evolving Position* (Berrien Springs, Mich.: Andrews Univ., 1993).

6. In addition to *WGM*, Pinnock made brief, related statements on this subject in "Toward an Evangelical Theology of Religions," *Journal of the Evangelical Theological Society* 33 (1990): 359–68; and at the emotionally energized 1989 Evangelical Theological Society annual meeting in San Diego, California.

7. For instance, I do not deal with Pinnock's doctrine of hell, though my criticisms have essential implications for that doctrine. Recent evangelical treatments of modern interpretations of hell are found in Larry Dixon, *The Other Side of the Good News: Confronting The Contemporary Challenges to Jesus' Teaching on Hell* (Wheaton, Ill.: Victor Books-BridgePoint, 1992), who specifically deals with Pinnock's views; and Ajith Fernando, *Crucial Questions About Hell* (Eastbourne, Sussex, England: Kingsway, 1991).

8. I agree with Sanders that "enough information does exist for the construction of a biblically satisfying and theologically sound answer" (*NON*, 17) against those who propose that we must pursue a healthy skepticism on

the matter. Although we could leave the matter where it really and finally rests—in God's mysterious sovereignty and fair justice—we must discuss revelatory information on the subject. We must also decide whether or not we will accept the information that exists. Harold O. J. Brown, in reviewing Pinnock's book writes, "There is no doubt that the situation as described by traditional orthodoxy is a bad situation. The important question is not: "Is it bad? but rather: Is it true?" (*Christianity Today*, 14 September 1992, 40).

9. For an excellent evangelical critique of Paul Knitter and John Hick, see Harold A. Netland, *Dissonant Voices: Religious Pluralism and the Question of Truth* (Grand Rapids: Eerdmans, 1991). See also Ken Gnanakan, *The Pluralist Predicament* (Bangalore: Theological Book Trust, 1992).

10. Carl E. Braaten, *No Other Gospel!: Christianity Among the World's Religions* (Minneapolis: Fortress, 1992), 18–24, identifies and illustrates these: Christian identity, rational intelligibility, and social applicability as "three types of theology" in his excellent first chapter, "American Protestantism Lacks a Reformation."

1

INCLUSIVISM: A PRELIMINARY DIALOGUE

The first submission of this book was written with the professional theologian in mind. However, the publisher wanted me to popularize the style. It was then I was introduced to *Key Grammar Checker* (Softkey Software Products. Macmillan, 1990. Remarks here are from opening pages of the program manual.). This is a software program that deals with syntax, structure, and style for modern business writing. Its "overall critique" of my literary attempt agreed with the human editors. I had failed in "readability." Readers needed a fifth-grade level of writing for best readability and I had achieved an eleventh-grade level. I had blundered in "sentence structure" with too many compound sentences (including this one) and subordinate clauses being used. To my relief, I somewhat passed the "strength index," which examines style of writing. However, I was intrigued by its analysis of *biblical* words such as punishment, judgment, condemnation, hell, death, and so on. To modern editors who put the software program together, these were "offensive" words in "negative" phrases. Unlike human editors, this grammar program was not busy, bored, or bellicose. As strongly as it could it immediately recommended that I use other words. I thought its recommendation was offensive and negative!

The upcoming dialogue with inclusivists resembles this "you too" interaction with the software program. I shall first introduce the axioms of inclusivism. Then, I shall indicate that inclusivists fall prey to their own analysis of exclusivist style, structure, and syntax.

OVERVIEW OF THE
INCLUSIVIST HYPOTHESIS[1]

Inclusivists contend that explicit knowledge of Jesus Christ in this earthly life is unnecessary for the eternal salvation of those who have not heard about Him. In this way, many more people can and will be included in divine salvation. An exclusive insistence that one must believe on the Lord Jesus to be saved is considered too restrictive. God can and will save more people than "the fewness doctrine" that evangelicalism has traditionally espoused. Evangelicals, inclusivists say, must come to terms with the present realities[2] in which the masses of the world find themselves. A competent, evangelical theology of religions[3] is needed. Inclusivists offer their theology of religions as an option for evangelical consideration. It is built on two critical axioms.

Universality Axiom

The first axiom finds an "optimism of salvation" toward the unevangelized in the gracious, universal love of God.[4] The universal orientation of the early chapters of Genesis; the "global covenants" with Noah and Abraham; and the "pagan saint" feature as seen in Melchizedek, Abimelech, and others, prove that "God works outside so-called salvation history" (*WGM*, 27). The election of Israel through Abraham was to serve God's global reach as seen in "God's dialogue with the nations" in the rest of the Old Testament. In the gospels, though Jesus was sent primarily to Israel, "one should not confuse penultimate means with ultimate ends" (*WGM*, 31). The epistles and Revelation, too, show God's boundless generosity. And if "God really loves the whole world and desires everyone to be saved, it follows logically that everyone must have access to salvation" (*WGM*, 157).

Particularity Axiom

The second axiom is Christological: "the finality of Jesus as the decisive manifestation and ground of God's grace toward sinners" (*WGM*, 49). In a tight and clear apologetic, Pinnock argues for a high Christology "without forgetting that the uniqueness of Jesus derives from Israel's God" (*WGM*, 53). Jesus' derived uniqueness is especially seen in Jesus' claims and His audience's responses to Him. Pinnock concludes this section with "it is propositionally the case that Jesus is definitively and unsurpassably the Lord of the universe" (*WGM*, 63).

Ramifications of the Axioms

The "high Christology" axiom is related to the "optimism-of-salvation" axiom by commending the spirit and the wisdom of the Second Vatican Council. "There is no salvation except through Christ but it is not necessary for everybody to possess a conscious knowledge of Christ in order to benefit from redemption through him" (*WGM*, 75).

As a result of relating the two axioms, it is alleged that some pet evangelical doctrines need to be revised in the direction of inclusivism. The ramifications of this relationship are as follows. One must distinguish the ontological necessity for Christ's work of redemption from the epistemological situation of sinners. "Ontological necessity" means that Jesus Christ is decisive as the ground of one's salvation. People's "epistemological situation" relates to their ignorance about Christ. So, inclusivists assert that Jesus is decisive as the ground of one's salvation, but not necessary as the content of one's faith. "God has more going on by way of redemption than what happened in first century Palestine, decisive though that was for the salvation of the whole world" (*WGM*, 77). So faith explicitly in Christ is not critical for salvation. The unevangelized may seek God apart from Jesus Christ and still be saved. Salvation comes within the reach of the evangelized by the "faith principle"— the basis of universal accessibility (*WGM*, 157). The faith principle is seen in Hebrews 11:6, fleshed out in the "holy pagan" tradition, the presence of believing Jews before Christ, Cornelius "the believer in God before he became a Christian" (*WGM*, 165), the mentally incompetent, and babies who die in infancy. All these show "many varieties of unevangelized will attain salvation" (*WGM*, 168).

The theological basis for this position arises from a trinitarian doctrine of redemption (*WGM*, 79) and prevenient grace,[5] the comprehensive activity of the Logos, Israelite borrowing from Near Eastern religions, the salvific mediation of general revelation, and the existence of the word for "God" denoting the Supreme Being all over the world (*WGM*, 97).

So, on the one hand, non-Christians may "make a faith response to God in the form of actions of love and justice" (ibid.).

On the other hand, Christians are Messianic believers who have found full-strength salvation in Jesus. "But responding to premessianic revelation can make them (non-Christians) right with God" (*WGM*, 105). Just as God gets through to people in the course of secular life, home life, work life, and other experiences, He does not absent Himself completely from the religious sphere (*WGM*, 108).

Further, postmortem salvation is available for those who could not decide for salvation before death. "One group that will have a grace-filled postmortem encounter with Christ consists of those who sought God during their earthly lives and loved him, though they had not heard of Jesus" (*WGM*, 171). Finally, inclusivism does not stultify missions because it broadens the incentive beyond the traditionally narrow evangelical motivation for doing missions, which is merely to help provide deliverance from wrath (*WGM*, 177).

A CRITIQUE OF INCLUSIVIST PURPOSES AND MOTIVATIONS

Our preliminary critique looks at three stated motivations to Pinnock's book, made by the author himself. My criticisms, at the level of motivations, will also contain a couple of appropriate comments. We acknowledge the usual liability of such argumentation. However, I need to employ them justifiably to uncover the confusion that necessarily relates to the soundness of inclusivist arguments.

Historical/Cultural Relativity

As indicated above, inclusivists challenge a hardline restrictivism that insists that one must "exercise explicit faith in Jesus Christ in this earthly life" (*WGM*, 12) to encounter God. Restrictivism, they claim, exhibits a "pessimism of salvation" with the main motivation for missions being the rescue of people from the fate of hell. An attitude of "optimism of salvation" is what "we need if we are to deal with the challenge of other religions" (*WGM*, 13).

A part of Pinnock's argument is guided by modern sensibilities against the positions of exclusivist evangelicalism.[6] Conditioned by these sensibilities, anything hardline and pessimistic that leads to harsh conclusions (cf. his comments, *WGM*, 51) becomes unacceptable. For the most part, Pinnock's need for optimism is not so much an argument as it is a preference. That is, he has simply assumed and not established the biblical, theological, or philosophical superiority of "optimistic" notions over "pessimistic" notions. There is no doubt that culturally and historically, modern sentiment prefers optimism to pessimism, moderation to harshness, inclusivism to exclusivism, and positive thinking to negative thinking. And as the challenge of world religions drives Pinnock to an optimistic interpretive framework, he attempts to find biblical material to fortify such a cultural and historical preference. There is hardly any serious treatment of the harsh, severe, and negative passages of Scripture. He is anxious to communicate what exhausts God's love, but there is no mention about what exhausts God's wrath. He would also like to show that "high Christology does not entail a narrow outlook" (*WGM*, 51), because narrowness causes problems for interreligious dialogue and positive relationships with non-Christians. Hermeneutical adjustments are made to fit present historical and cultural preferences. We do not disagree that an ideology of "manyness" emotionally satisfies, even as an ideology of "fewness" emotionally repels those who want large numbers to be saved. However, to build important doctrines driven by either ideology exposes both to similar and justified criticisms.

This preceding observation is similar to the inclusivist ascription of historical factors to the development and reinforcement of the "restrictivist model" that "restricts hope to people who have put their faith in Jesus Christ in this earthly life" (*WGM*, 14–15). "With Augustine a new and severe paradigm in theology was born, a package of dismal beliefs which would eat its way into the consciousness of the Western churches and erode the positive biblical spirit in their thinking" (*WGM*, 39). Historical factors—"the enemies of the state automatically became enemies of Christianity as well" (*WGM*, 37), along with theological factors—"the bitter Pelagian controversy" (*WGM*, 38), are said to have originated or hardened "the fewness doctrine." Luther and Calvin followed Augustine's trend. But, similar to this historical, theological megashift that generated restrictivism, recently a more positive, generous spirit is evident "and is being increasingly shared by conservative evangelicals as well" (*WGM*, 41). When one reads Pinnock's head chapter, a "positive biblical spirit" toward salvific optimism, based on an inclusivist selection of Scriptures, becomes *theologically* preferable to negative restrictivism.[7]

A couple of observations may be made about the issue of historical and cultural influence and the ensuing relativity. First, the notion of a "paradigm shift" has been used to advance novel ideas in varied fields from scientific revolutions to market research to theological thinking.[8] The theory is that the happening of a revolution does not relate to startling new facts as much as the overall way in which the universe is seen.[9] The particular revolution may be for reasons that have little to do with the internal logic of the discipline and a lot to do with the society in which scientists and theologians live and work. That is, the revolutionary shift tells us more about the person offering the theory and the world in which he lives than what the theory itself proposes.

In terms of our topic, Pinnock's application of the "paradigm shift" idea to and from the Augustinian restrictivist model elicits a return criticism. He falls to his own criticism of Augustine's historical conditioning, for in all of this, the dogmas that supposedly escape historical and cultural relativity are his own counter proposals, as well as any statements concerning such relativity. We find this feature in a somewhat more audacious historical observation, "God is correcting a mistake in historical theology by means of historical factors, combined with a fresh reading of Scripture" (*WGM*, 42). How Pinnock has access to this divine corrective and extra-biblical reading of history is in itself a reasonable question. But why this corrected reading could not and would not be "divinely" corrected again in the future also needs to be addressed by him. D. Pailin astutely remarks:

> The problem of theologians is that of finding a way by which they may become aware of their own culture's values sufficiently to recognize how those values condition their theological understanding and critically to assess that conditioning. It is often easy to see the cultural relativity of theologies developed in other cultures and to admit in principle that our own must be similarly relative. What is difficult is to find ways of identifying and evaluating that relativity in our own understanding.[10]

Inclusivists are anxious to explain the conditioned origin of the restrictivist model, without being self-critically aware of the conditioned character of their own thought.[11]

Second, there is a major difference between science and theology in the application of the "paradigm" paradigm. Evangelical theologians work with a closed canon (completed Bible) for investigation of a finite amount of scriptural data, with limitations in the scope of their meaning. In some issues at least, Scriptures do not permit the open-ended, never-certain, always-varying relativity that accompanies scientific enquiry. We agree that new historical and cultural environments ask new questions to which the Bible responds. But the nature of Scripture is not and was not its own limitation. The presumed limitation of Scripture is traced to the theologian's ignorance of the new questions that a new and different environment asks of Scripture. As this book progresses, we will see that the pluralistic climate that faces evangelical theologians does not obligate Scripture to yield to the revision of evangelical soteriology and the reduction of evangelical Christology that inclusivists recommend.[12]

Theological Responsibility

Pinnock purposes to put together an *evangelical* theology of religions in writing his book. "There is nothing like this at present, so it will be my aim to provide such a proposal."[13] Earlier he writes, "For two millennia the church has proclaimed the finality of Jesus Christ as the Savior of the world, but recently people have been asking exactly how this works" (*WGM*, 7).

The tenor of these statements appears to assume too much responsibility. Sensitive theologians in cultures with non-Christian majorities have no option but to deal with the matter of religions. The outlines of an evangelical theology of religions emerge each time they meet or write.[14]

It is improper for Pinnock to think that evangelicals have not asked and answered questions about the topic for two millennia. The word *recently* shows a residual, theological colonialism that does not allow Western theologians to admit seriously that non-Western thinkers and missionaries have had to wrestle with the theological and existential aspects of this precise problem for centuries.[15] Elsewhere Pinnock writes, "There are different reasons why Christians have felt threatened by the existence of other religions in the past and have found it difficult to relate lovingly to them. These would include geographical isolation" (*WGM*, 19). Non-Western Christians have simply not been geographically isolated from this critical theological and social issue.

Pinnock (and North American evangelicals at large) need to learn from those who live and witness in non-Christian majority cultures. It would have been facile theologically, biblically, and existentially for non-Western evangelicals to make inclusivist adjustments to the Scriptures. Could inclusivists give some respect to why those evangelicals have not propounded an inclusivist theory in context-sensitive evangelism in pluralistic environments? Such a study would provide illuminating theological and interesting sociological insights for Pinnock (and the rest of us) on this crucial matter.

For example, take "The Seoul Declaration: Towards An Evangelical Theology for the Third World" (contained in Ro and Eshenaur, 21–27). It declares that the first matter for *Asian* evangelical thinking is the resurgence of indigenous religions. Hear these thinkers write about their theological task: "The distinctive Asian qualities of spirituality, meditation, devotion, self-sacrifice and servanthood are to be tested and utilized in developing our theology" (ibid., 25). Nothing is said or made of favorite *Asian* themes such as religious pluralism, functional relativism, and soteriological inclusivism as providing the data or the parameters for evangelical "grappling." This glaring omission by an influential and formal evangelical declaration from the non-West cannot be written off as a "conservative refusal to think" (*WGM*, 11), or as some socio-psychological slip of Western-trained, non-Western evangelical theologians. For good theological reasons, non-Western evangelicals have maintained the finality, exclusivity, necessity, and sufficiency of Jesus Christ for all peoples. Pinnock's desire for "greater theological globalism" (*WGM*, 12) would and should include evangelical reflections from the non-Western world.

These social problems are simply newer in the West where "religious pluralism has always been present but not always in a context that leans towards relativism regarding truth claims" (*WGM*, 11). The multiplicity of religions and a pluralistic mindset forms an influential sociological grid for many non-Western nations. Could "open-minded" evangelicals in the West learn from "closed-minded" evangelicals elsewhere? As far as I know, almost all non-Western evangelicals recognize "positive ways in which religions contribute to human well being" (*WGM*, 12). Indeed, they have learned the rudiments and practice of indigenous life from the ethical truths and the wise input of local religions. However, their primary theological hesitation relates to non-Christian religions as channels of eternal salvation outside of depending in this life on the Lord Jesus Christ as the Only God and Savior of all men.

Individualism

Pinnock desires to correct a Western, individualistic view on salvation and judgment (while not "stretching the corporate emphasis too far," which he claims contributes too much to evangelical soteriological beliefs (*WGM*, 151–53). However, we notice that his criticism of Western individualism does not prohibit him from a similar individualistic, entrepreneurial enthusiasm in his own motivations. While claiming to be "an orthodox theologian" (*WGM*, 40), he attempts through biblical exposition, theological argument, and historical support to convince evangelicals of the legitimacy of a fringe position.[16] He also desires to "draw out greater support for the broader outlook from a significant number" of "scholars who have remained silent on these issues for fear of criticism" (*WGM*, 181). Earlier, he hopes "to nudge fellow evangelicals who have so far been reluctant to speak out, owing to the intimidation they may feel from hardline restrictivists" (*WGM*, 13).

Of course, it is an unrecognized "Western individualism" that keeps him inventive without regard or allegiance to the minority, historical Christian community called evangelicalism in many parts of the world. M. Noll's remarks show up Pinnock's motivations as a classic illustration of some aspects of North American evangelicalism:

> This antitraditional attitude creates a number of problems for the evangelical study of Scripture. It is one of the things that robs evangelicals of an historical sense. And this is a debilitating handicap when one is attempting to understand an ancient text. . . . For Bible scholars the danger is twofold. It is all too easy to allow forms of thought which appear to be only common sense in our century, but which are largely foreign to the world of Scripture, to dictate interpretations of what the biblical writers must have intended. But it is also a temptation for scholars to let the valid fruits of their empathetic research languish for fear of upsetting the dearly held commonsensical opinions of the wider evangelical community.[17]

Although he is unbridled in overcoming the second danger cited by Noll, Pinnock succumbs to the first danger.

Pinnock also displays a Western, individualistic ruggedness in other areas. His dismissal of the epistemological necessity of Jesus is an evangelically odd doctrine. The argument with Pinnock concerns his ardent aspiration to stand with, find out, or encourage a few evangelicals who may quietly hold to the ontological need and the epistemological non-need of Jesus for salvation (cf. citation in *WGM*, 181 n. 52) while ignoring the many evangelicals who openly (and unfortunately, arrogantly) hold to the exclusivist view of salvation.[18]

Further, the individualism he criticizes really necessitates stating the premise that this entire book seeks to challenge: an egalitarian entitlement and opportunity for all *individuals* to hear the gospel. Pinnock also applies such an individualism to non-Western communities. "There is enough truth in most religions for people to take hold of and put their trust in God's mercy. The religion may help or hinder—*but ultimately it is what the person decides that counts.*"[19]

Exchanges and interchanges like the one in which we have just engaged may be classified as "toward the man" or ad hominem arguments. Again, these dialogues are oriented to the thinker rather than the thoughts he has proposed. They do not precisely deal with the issues at hand, but they carry incidental weight in argumentation. That is why both sides of the inclusivism/exclusivism debate indulge in the limited fancies of ad hominem reasoning.

We next move to a more substantive conversation with the axioms and implications of soteriological inclusivism that at first encounter may appeal to an evangelical constituency—the hermeneutical foundations of inclusivism.

Notes

1. I recommend your reading of either inclusivist (Pinnock, *WGM*, or Sanders, *NON;* see Bibliography), to correct any unintentional misrepresentation (by emphasis or omission) of their positions on my part, and for your firsthand understanding of their arguments. Their main reasoning and conclusions are recapitulated in the ensuing section. Interaction with the overview arises in the review later in this chapter.

2. The Canadian pluralistic environment, where Christianity is being displaced from prominence and is thus being threatened, is a key element affecting Pinnock's theological concern (*WGM*, 10).

3. Pinnock is to be complimented for jarring Western evangelical minds into putting the issue on the forefront of theological discussion. "I hope it might place the issue of religious pluralism on the agenda of evangelical theology for the nineties, the way the Lausanne Covenant placed social concerns on the evangelical agenda for the seventies. The time is right" (*WGM*, 15).

4. Sanders refers to this axiom as the "universal salvific will" of God" as suggested in passages such as 1 Timothy 2:3–4 (*NON*, 25).

5. *WGM*, 76. "God the Father is present everywhere in his graciousness, not only where Jesus of Nazareth is named. God is present and at work in every sphere of human life secular as well as sacred" (p. 76). Wesleyan prevenient grace is roughly equal to Calvinist common grace. Either way, "it means that the grace of God mitigates the effects of sin in human life and preserves the creature from self-destruction" (p. 103).

6. While the "offence taken" by him is traceable through the early part of the book, it is highly evident in his discussion of "The Destruction of the Finally Impenitent," *Criswell Theological Review* 4 (Spring 1990): 243–59.

7. Pinnock's solution to historical/cultural influence probably agrees with Jeffery Hopper (*Understanding Modern Theology II: Reinterpreting Christian Faith for Changing Worlds* [Philadelphia: Fortress, 1987], 23ff.), who "makes plain" the fact of historical and cultural relativity in doctrinal formulation. (This delicate approval of Hopper's article is found in Pinnock's "The Destruction of the Finally Impenitent," 243, n. 1.)

   If all doctrinal formulations portray and exhibit historical and cultural relativity, Hopper rightly asks the consequent "relativity of all truth" question concerning the "*nature* of the *truth* that theology seeks to express" (p. 26). Hopper then advances a problem-prone position, "The suggestion of a nonpropositional understanding of theological truth would be that the truth is not in the doctrines themselves, but in the faith-relationship that those doctrines may help to make possible for some people" (p. 27). Again Hopper notes, "the truth does not inhere in the doctrines but in the reality experienced by persons of faith" (p. 28). Also, "For the recognition of the fact of historical and cultural relativity helps one to realize that real confidence cannot come from placing radical trust—even implicitly—in our doctrines. Such trust belongs only to God, and God remains transcendent" (p. 29).

   These comments from Hopper constitute a premonitory outline of Pinnock's book. Pinnock's "faith-principle" discharges Christians from significant responsibility to particular, propositional content obligated by the claims in the historical circumstance of Jesus Christ. The transcendent God-beyond-Jesus could be related to in radical trust, regardless of worldview differences on the nature of God. And for Pinnock, truth inheres in the reality of the faith experience.

8. A stimulating discussion on paradigm change in theology and science is found in Hans Kung, *Theology for the Third Millennium: An Ecumenical View* (New York: Doubleday, 1988), 123–69.

9. See Thomas S. Kuhn, *The Structure of Scientific Revolutions* (Chicago: Univ. of Chicago, 1962).

10. David A. Pailin, *The Anthropological Character of Theology: Conditioning Theological Understanding* (Cambridge, England: Cambridge Univ., 1990), 48.

11. We agree with T. C. Oden who notes that the purpose of Christian teaching is to "set forth the cohesive central tradition of the general consent of believers to apostolic teaching" and that "We should be doggedly pledged to irrelevance when relevance implies a corrupt indebtedness to modernity" (p. 203). Citing the anathema of Galatians 1:8–9, Oden makes a passionate plea "to commit ourselves to make no new contribution to theology" (p. 200). From "On Not Whoring After the Spirit of the Age," in *No God But God: Breaking with the Idols of Our Age,* ed. Os Guiness and John Seel (Chicago: Moody, 1992), 189–203.

12. Cf. the applicability of the Kuhn study to theology and historiography as evaluated in G. Cutting, *Paradigms and Revolutions: Appraisals and Applications of Thomas Kuhn's Philosophy of Science* (South Bend, Ind.: Univ. of Notre Dame Press, 1980), from a non-evangelical perspective.

13. *WGM,* 13. Less evangelically debatable proposals are affirmed in his "Toward an Evangelical Theology of Religions," *Journal of the Evangelical Theological Studies* 33 (1990): 359–68.

14. For a bibliographic beginning, one may consult several works found in the Selected Bibliography of *The Bible and Theology in Asian Contexts,* ed. Bong Rin Ro and Ruth Eshenaur (Bangalore: Association of Evangelical Theological Education in India, 1984), 395–98.

15. An excellent source of point and counterpoint in interreligious relations where evangelical thinkers and missionaries were involved during the 1800s in India is found in Richard Fox Young, *Resistant Hinduism: Sanskrit Sources on Anti-Christian Apologetics in Early Nineteenth-Century India* (Vienna: Institut fur Indologie der Universitat Wien, 1981). The other necessary orbit of theological interaction by non-Western thinkers is in the area of Christian social responsibility in the face of economic deprivation.

16. Sanders provides the research basis, in the following order, for six views on the destiny question: key biblical texts, theological considerations for the position, leading defenders, evaluation, and a historical bibliography. Pinnock goes one step further than Sanders's analyses to positively explore pertinent issues in the context of religions and Christology. Both speak to the need of missions in light of their revisions (cf. Pinnock in *WGM,* 176–80; and Sanders in *NON,* 284–86; 262–63).

17. Mark Noll, "Evangelicals and the Study of the Bible," in *Evangelicalism and Modern America,* ed. George Marsden (Grand Rapids: Eerdmans, 1984), 117–18.

18. His broader motivation is also ecumenical: "Optimism of salvation enjoys such a broad biblical basis that it can be negotiated smoothly. Roman Catholics, Lutherans, Calvinists, Wesleyans, Pentecostals—all of them can make the shift to greater universality in their own way while dealing with the special challenges their tradition creates" (*WGM,* 42).

19. *WGM*, 111 (italics added). One of the problems of the objective/subjective distinction in religion (which Pinnock makes in following W. C. Smith, *The Meaning and End of Religion* [New York: Macmillan, 1962], with subjective religion referring to the "human existential process of an individual's quest for meaning") is that it exhibits the wrong side of the individualism that Pinnock seeks to discount, and it affirms the traditional evangelical insistence of personal faith in Jesus Christ. Cultural anthropologists, church growth specialists, and missiologists have spoken to the individual-community relationship in the decision-making process. They often hold community decisions to be as valid as Western, individual ones. For example, see James P. Spradley, *The Ethnographic Interview* (New York: Holt, Rinehart and Winston, 1979), chap. 1, "Ethnography and Culture," for implications of this issue in finding cultural meaning systems in complex societies; or G. Linwood Barney, "Is Decision by Consensus Valid?", *The Alliance Witness*, 20 January 1971, 9–10.

We must also mention the role of the different concept of "self" in the theoretical religious frameworks as an additional complication in the relation of objective and subjective religion (cf. Lynn A. DeSilva, "The Problem of the Self in Buddhism and Christianity," in *What Asian Christians Are Thinking*, ed. Douglas Elwood (Cleveland: New Day, 1978). We will consider the validity and use of the distinction between objective and subjective religion later.

2

How Universal Is God's Mercy?

Key Grammar Checker, my software program, also recommended that I use the active voice to strengthen my writing. I wanted to use a "he too" retort to subvert and soften this undeniable analysis because the inclusivists' quotations in this chapter were rated the same way. Nevertheless, I took heed of the software's recommendation as I rewrote the manuscript for this book.

Consider some observations on writing style. Writing preferences are not absolute. A person's style may be active or passive, and therefore impactful or flat for certain audiences. Style is therefore a relative matter, and one can truly be a pluralist when it comes to literary style.

Although style cannot be judged right or wrong, a person's substance can be evaluated that way, or at least as mostly right or mostly wrong. Why? When there is a definite criterion of truth and error to which a person appeals and calls another position wrong and his own correct on the basis of that criterion, he too may be evaluated upon that same definite standard.

Our conversation with inclusivism now moves into the range of substantive issues. So far I have examined only secondary issues of purposes and motivations—similar to the software's concerns about my writing style. We now proceed "toward the idea," (ad reu, rather than ad hominem). The topic of Jesus Christ's salvation and its critical orbit of issues for the Christian faith are to be broached, defined, and evaluated by the Scriptures. In conceptual proposals, there is often difficulty in discriminating between what is axiomatic and what is implicational or applicational. However, as mentioned in the preliminary dialogue, the axioms of inclusivism have already been furnished for our consideration.

THE UNIVERSALITY AXIOM

The universality axiom shows God's commitment to "full racial salvation" (*WGM*, 19). Derived from a hermeneutics of hope which italicizes the universal emphases of the Bible (*WGM*, 20f.), this axiom commends an optimism of salvation toward those who have not heard the gospel. This axiom basically governs inclusivists' reading of the Scriptures with regard to the extent of salvation. My investigation here examines the biblical arguments for the universality axiom.

OLD TESTAMENT MISSIOLOGY

The universal intention of God's salvation can be easily discerned from a missiological reading of the Old Testament.[1] Our questions relate to using these Old Testament missiological indicators to extract the inclusivist viewpoint.

It is obvious that God's focus began with all of humanity before it came more specifically to the Hebrews. There is no doubt that God's global heart is confirmed in the early chapters of Genesis. However, the issue is whether or not these passages evidencing salvation outside the stream of the Abrahamic line can be used to present God's large "saving plan" (*WGM*, 21), as inclusivists suggest, or simply to establish God's global largeheartedness from the very beginning of human history. Here God's "saving plan" from the "global covenants" (*WGM*, 20) of Genesis has to be mentioned too. Pinnock admits that this optimism-of-salvation-reading of the Scriptures "does not . . . yield a lot of specific details" (*WGM*, 47; Sanders, too, after attempting a rather strong support for the wider hope from the Old Testament, writes, "there was little explicit teaching about that in the Old Testament" [*NON*, 37]). Yet Pinnock adds theological details to fill the supposed gaps.

In the study that follows, one will notice conclusions that are counter to the inclusivist conclusion concerning the Old Testament period of salvation history. We will see that a major obstacle to the large saving plan of God in early Genesis is the open characterization of a retributive God of judgment along with a clearly stated "fewness doctrine" of salvation. We shall also see that even if the early Genesis passages are read with an international focus, they do not characterize a generic, faith commitment to a(ny) theistic God, as inclusivists hope. Further, an international saving focus from Genesis 1–11 does not necessarily lead to nor theologically entail a pattern of salvation outside or before Jesus Christ for God-believers after the incarnation of Jesus Christ.

The Creation Covenant

Old Testament support for inclusivism begins with creation. "We can speak of a covenant of creation such that the whole world and its peoples belong to God who created humanity to relate to him" (*WGM*, 20). However, a covenant with creation by the "creator and judge of all nations" (ibid.) also includes and implies man's accountability to this Maker who owns him. Notice that Adam and Eve, as the first and only humans, had to face an exclusive, probationary issue (Gen. 2:16–17), which when broken brought death. Also, Abel offered the "firstlings of his flock" (Gen. 4:4) in contrast to Cain, who did not recognize his accountability to God and divine ownership of his life. Because God was in direct conversation with Cain even after his failure, we infer precise revelatory content to that early divine-human relationship. These pre-Flood days show not only mercy but also judgments on all creation—nature (cf. the Edenic curse) and humans (cf. the curse, Cain's banishment and his godless line). The contribution this period makes to understanding the extent of God's salvation is His non-discriminatory (not equal opportunity or accessibility) stance toward mercy (Abel, Enoch, Noah; *WGM*, 22) and judgment (cf. the earliest genealogy-based obituary in Genesis 5), based on special revelation. Actually, the content of revelation to Abel, Enoch, and Noah (as found in Hebrews 11) is *specific.* (Hebrews 11:6 is a pivotal passage for the inclusivist proof of a generic "faith-principle" in the Old Testament. See below.) Abel obtained the *testimony of his righteousness,* God testifying about his gifts (v. 4). Enoch obtained the witness before he was taken up that he was pleasing to God. Noah had been warned by God about things not yet seen . . . and became an heir of righteousness (v. 7). (Pinnock's inclusion of Daniel in this list "prior to the call of Abraham" [*WGM*, 22] seems to be mistaken.)

Old Testament Name-Theology. Genesis 4:26 has an important theme that runs throughout Scripture. The theme which, while adding or specifying content in the course of incremental revelation, became sustained and specific. To use inclusivist terminology, the "faith principle" for salvation in this period was the "calling upon or proclaiming or naming[2] the name of the YHWH." "In critical and chronic need man realized the full effects of the curse and began to call on God's name—Gen. 4:26."[3] This specification of a name is influential in the development of a "name-theology" background for the New Testament apostolic use of the term name. YHWH was not an unnamed, generic object of prayer or worship for those early humans.[4] YHWH as creator could be called on by all humans before the name became a nationalistic claim.

The "YHWH" contribution to Old Testament "name-theology" begins in the early chapters of Genesis. There is a seeming difficulty with Exodus 6:2–3 where God says that by His name (YHWH) He did not make Himself known to Abraham, Isaac, and Jacob, but appeared as "God Almighty" (El Shaddai). However, the name YHWH appears throughout the book of Genesis from the very beginning. On this supposed problem, W. C. Kaiser notes:

> The solution lies in the Niphal reflexive verbs in Ex. 6:2–3 and the Beth Essentia before El Shaddai and its extended force before Yahweh. The resulting affirmation made in the text is that God claims, "I manifested myself in the character of [Beth Essentiae] El Shaddai, but in *the character* [*Beth Essentiae* implied] Yahweh, I did not make myself known to them.[5]

In the Exodus passage, El Shaddai was the primary name by which the patriarchs knew God and His character. Now He was going to make Himself known to them in the character of YHWH. In any case, my point is that in this incipient stage of pre-Jewish and human history, YHWH as a "name" had identity and specification with minimal *character* content. His fuller identity and character were to be revealed in Exodus 3:13 (cf. "what," not "who," thus asking for character as well as identity) and throughout the Old Testament. YHWH's fullest identity and character will come in the Lord Jesus Christ.

So this named and identified deity began early in human history. The faith principle in any God—without or with another name; unknown or unknowable—is unsustainable from these passages. The "calling upon the *name* of the Lord" is the pre-Flood (Gen. 4:26); post-Flood (Abraham, Gen. 12:8); Israelite (Jer. 33:3); Christian (Rom. 10:13); and eschatological (Joel 2:32) condition for deliverance. It is a necessary and epistemological condition for God's intervention in human history. The Genesis writer notes that Enoch (Gen. 5:22) and Noah (Gen. 6:9) walked with *God.* Assuming a unified view of Pentateuchal authorship, the Lord on whom people called was the God with whom they walked. Salvation was through a "faith-in-YHWH principle" for all peoples.[6]

A Global Judgment. This early time period culminates with the massive outpouring of God's wrath on the whole world. In discussing Noah, it is incongruous that Pinnock does not mention the judgment which takes place in Noah's time. How anyone can miss or ignore this dominant, worldwide judgment in the text is difficult to grasp. While looking for those included in salvation, we must take into account those who are excluded from it. Those included in this global judgment fit the categories of people who are candidates for a coming global judgment. Active and passive rejecters of God (and that so many of them) were left out of an earthly (and/or wholistic) salvation during the Flood. If the "restrictivist *fewness* doctrine" needs to be biblically verified, it is clearly observable at the Flood. All flesh is destroyed except for Noah, his sons, their wives, and the animals on the ark. The fewness doctrine was certainly in effect in the preservation of just eight righteous souls. A "manyness doctrine" of a sobering variety applied to the rest of humanity who were excluded from the safety of the ark. Also, most of those who should have heard Noah's message were not in geographical proximity to Noah. Neither does it seem that all willfully rejected Noah's message. They unknowingly ignored Noah but were still judged. Further, Jesus uses "Noah's day" to speak of judgment and not salvation (Matt. 24:36–41; cf. Luke 17:37, which provides Jesus' interpretation of the event). On this event, Hebrews 11:7 has a manyness doctrine of *condemnation.* In fear and faith "Noah prepared an ark for the salvation of his household, by which he condemned the *world.*" Eventually, no one was spared except for the preacher of righteousness and his family who entered into the exclusive ark.

The inclusivist conclusion from this early set of Scripture that "there are true believers in the wider world who trust God and walk faithfully before Him" (*WGM*, 22) can be called to task on two accounts. One, there was no "wider" and "narrower" world of believers at this period of time. The world of believers was as wide as it was at its narrowest and as narrow as it was at its widest. And two, even if inclusivists want to posit wide and narrow worlds of believers (two categories of the saved), this historical period and Scriptural passages permit only one category. A general "faith response" to any deity other than YHWH is not a valid, timeless principle derivable from this period of salvation history.

The Noahic Covenant

Noah's safety was contingent on the faith acceptance of exclusive revelatory content given to him. Noah did according to *all that God commanded him* (Gen. 6:22). God's relationship to Noah displays a significant quantity of divine communication and quality of existential intimacy (6:9, 13). To use Noah for inclusivist purposes will depend on how much special revelation is sanctioned for the unevangelized today. Noah cannot be used for purposes of general revelation's mediating saving grace, unless general revelation is given specific content, in which case it is a subset of special revelation.

A Global Covenant. We well recognize that the Noahic covenant is a globally oriented covenant. It is true that evangelicals have interpreted "the Noahic covenant in a minimalist way and to see it as a covenant only of physical preservation and not of redemption" (*WGM*, 21). The reason for that physicalist interpretation, of course, is that the text seems to call for that. In Genesis 8:21 God promises that He will never again destroy every living thing. God also commits Himself to Noah and his descendants thus: "all flesh and the earth shall never again be cut off by the water of the flood" (9:11, 15). The point of the covenant—physical preservation—was the point of the Flood—the physical destruction of all flesh upon the earth. A globally oriented *redemption*-covenant is not in the picture. But it was a globally, not a personally or nationally, oriented covenant. This explains why though Noah is personally cursed for his indiscretion soon after (9:25), the covenant is kept. His descendants are party to the global covenant.

Racial Extermination. It is also obvious that "the promise to Noah prepares the way for the blessing of all nations through

Abram a few chapters later" (ibid.). Noah becomes the father of the entire race to whom the command to multiply is repeated. Genesis 10 is the fulfillment of that command, for nations and peoples come from Noah and his sons.

However, even though God's interest was the whole world, His work among the peoples was not merely redemptive. From Ham came Canaan whom Noah cursed. This was not the curse of simply an individual, but a prophetic curse of an entire line from Ham (cf. 10:6). Canaanite debauchery and depravity would later bring the extermination of that whole race by Israel (cf. Deut. 7:1–5). The extermination was not fully implemented, but the Canaanite race was dominated by Israel (Josh. 16:10; 17:12–13) and was a spiritual test to Israel (cf. the book of Judges). Concerning Canaan, even a "fewness doctrine" of salvation was not to be held by the Israelites. Sadly, it seems like a divine commitment to full racial extermination.

This double feature of salvation and judgment shows that even as salvation was before and outside the Israelite nation, there was severity as well. We must make sense of both routes of biblical thought on divine pronouncement and activity. All nations are from God. No nation is salvifically preferred for its own sake. These nations are neither accidental nor incidental to God's movement in history. God chooses to save or judge according to His purposes, and by sheer numbers more are slanted toward judgment than salvation.

International Confusion. If the Noahic covenant was global in scope, so was the effect of the Tower of Babel. The generation of Babel forgot to call upon the name of the Lord. Members of that generation forgot the flood of destruction. They wanted to make a name for themselves (Gen. 11:5). However, before they deserved another kind of global destruction (another flood had been ruled out), God, in His grace and judgment, sent a confusion of language and dispersed them. Although God would eventually use this diversity and multiplicity for His gracious purposes, the Babel-event was another debacle in human history. Pinnock mentions nothing of the Babel-event. The seeking and saving God of the universality axiom is also the "shattering and scattering"[7] God who disdains human hubris. The God who unifies and binds human communities is also the God who undoes and breaks human behavior.

Here is the inclusivist conclusion drawn from Genesis 1–11: "From the earliest chapters of the Bible we learn a fundamental (if neglected) truth, that salvation history is coextensive with world history and its goal of healing of all the nations" (*WGM*, 23). However, the most inclusivists can do with these chapters is hold that salvation history is coextensive with world history as far as time but not indiscriminate as far as constituents. That is, regardless of temporal or geographical location, people have been saved and have access to salvation based on specific faith-content. Not only are the judgment scenarios left out in inclusivist discussion of Genesis 1–11, it is rather ironic that the very few who have been named to salvation during this extended and unmeasured period of human history are used to construct a manyness doctrine of salvation from this passage of Genesis.

The Abrahamic Covenant

There is much missiologically useful material on the meaning of the Abrahamic covenant for the world. With the later Genesis and Pauline interpretations of the blessing of this covenant, one may prefer the passive or reflexive interpretations of "bless." By Abraham, the nations "shall be blessed" or "shall bless themselves." The means of divine blessing and the international dimensions of the promise to Abraham are clear. Abraham is a symbol and servant of God's universal heart. The Abrahamic call "designates the path God has chosen to bring about the salvation of the many through the faith of one, the principle of representation."[8]

If Noah could be used to show God's wider hope, Pinnock should have used Abraham as an example of true believers in the wider world. For after all, Abraham was not a Jew by birth and he came from a background of idolatry (cf. Josh. 24:2–3). Abraham's salvation from a pagan background disturbs the inclusivist hypothesis of salvation outside the Abrahamic stream of special revelation, for there was no such Abrahamic salvific tradition before Abraham.

Israel's Election. The election of Israel for the world is clear in her charter of existence (Ex. 19:6). Pinnock uses this corporate, elective significance in another way. "What a tragic and influential error. The Old Testament doctrine of election remains unchanged in the New Testament. The New Testament does not reinterpret election to mean the selection of certain individuals to be saved, leaving others aside" (*WGM*, 24).

I wish the comments on Israel's election could prove the point that inclusivists desire. There is no doubt that election became a nationalistic idol as Israel reinterpreted it for selfish ends, eventually rejecting YHWH's Son. And at other times when Israel forgot her elective responsibility (vocational purpose), the prophets were to remind the people. Election was not God *for* Israel *against* the world. It was God *for* Israel *for* the world.

Here is another statement on election that is difficult to sustain theologically or biblically. "Election has nothing to do with the eternal salvation of individuals but refers instead to God's way of saving the nations" (*WGM*, 25). The problem with this drastic bifurcation of personal-salvation and corporate-purpose dimensions of election is that all the non-Jewish illustrations of salvation cited from this time period are *individuals.* If election is corporate, in or to which group were these individuals elect? Also, what would be the vocational and missiological calling of believing non-Jews before Christ, if *Israel* was to be the corporate means for a vocational purpose? Further, if during the Old Testament all who were corporately and missiologically elect were also individually and salvifically elect, then all Israel would be saved for having been born as Jews. But for both inclusivists and exclusivists faith is necessary for salvation at all times during human history. Therefore, the evangelical stress in "turning" vocational election into a soteriological one is more fairly a mistake of emphasis rather than category. I, for one, think that this "turning" is more prone to happen in traditionally "Christian" nations. I even heard a missions motivation that emphasized a functional similarity between America and Israel because of the middle letters of JerUSAlem. The church in traditionally "Christian" nations seems to repeat Israel's mistaken elective idolatry. We have emphasized an election "from" (detachment) and an election "to" (attachment), but not election "for" (engagement) service.

As a doctrine that qualifies as a true biblical mystery, the "both-and" (instead of an "either-or") design of argument appears to integrally apply more to the election doctrine than any other single biblical doctrine. The "election" dimension is continuous through the testaments and has four dimensions: the corporate, personal, soteriological, and missiological. The corporate dimension has missiological intent (Ex. 19:6; 1 Peter 2:9: "A chosen race to proclaim God's excellencies," see also v. 5). The corporate dimension has a soteriological past and future (cf. Rom. 11:2, 26–27; cf. also 1 Peter 1:1–2 with 2 Peter 1:10–11). There is a personal dimension that has soteriological intent (Gal. 1:15, "set apart to reveal his son in me"). And, finally, there is a personal dimension that has missiological intent (Gal. 1:16; "that I might preach Him among the Gentiles"; cf. others personally chosen for missiological reasons: Abraham, Gen. 12:3; Isaac, Gen. 26:4; Jacob, Gen. 28:14). Election is both individual and corporate, loves and thus damns, includes and thus excludes, prefers and thus passes over, is soteriological and vocational, is a privilege and responsibility. These are not contradictory categories. Consequently, to set vocational and soteriological election at odds is not consistent with biblical data. (That is what Pinnock does: "What a mistake to have made vocational election into a soteriological category" [*WGM*, 25].)

Since biblical election is soterio-missiological, simply accenting soteriology over vocation does not yield the grounds toward a traditional fewness doctrine with double predestination ("where God by sovereign fiat decrees some to be saved and some to be condemned" [*WGM*, 24]) overtones. This is what Pinnock detects in the restrictivist argument (ibid., 30: "Bewitched by the alien doctrine of double predestination, we have overlooked the meaning of the call of Abraham"). On the other hand, to say that "election has nothing to do with the eternal salvation of individuals but refers to God's way of saving the nations" (*WGM*, 25) is a mistaken notion, too. To change the emphasis from individual to corporate in order to avoid casting "a deep shadow over the character of God" (ibid.) only raises individual propensities toward pride and arrogance to a corporate level.[9] The problem with the ideology of election is not related so much to the doctrine of election, but to that of human nature. The elect constantly seem to misinterpret election to reflect privilege rather than to see it as a responsibility to provide such salvation privileges to others. So, Israel misinterpreted its selection. The church too forgets that it was "chosen on behalf of many" (ibid.). Deeming election only as a vocational category does not adequately cover biblical data, and regarding election as a soteriological category does not rule out vocational responsibility. On both counts, the inclusivist view that election is only corporate and vocational is deficient.

The Melchizedek Factor. One of the stronger arguments for an inclusivist, wider-hope teaching is the Melchizedek narrative. "This incident in Genesis 14 makes the point that religious experience may be valid outside Judaism and Christianity" (*WGM*, 94). We need to consider this observation as well.

One problem with this view is that it refers to a time when neither Judaism nor Christianity existed. The Jewish race began with Abraham (cf. Deut. 26:5), but it was during Moses' time that the constitution of the nation and the principles of the religion were formalized. Pinnock's observation may be permitted to carry some weight *before* Judaism and Christianity existed, but it has no force if applied completely outside of and apart from either religion. Too, he needs to demonstrate that his assertion would be valid after the establishment of these biblical religions.

Now the "manyness" doctrine of salvation remains unproven when based on *occasional* instances such as Melchizedek. In Scripture, more people are saved in relation to the main stream of salvation from Abraham rather than outside it. These occasional instances definitely point to extraordinary, "divine revelatory initiatives."[10] But Melchizedek's knowledge of God was not qualitatively different, as to source or effect, from Enoch's, Noah's, and Abraham's, except that he was a rather mysterious figure.[11] None of these men came from an Abrahamite salvific tradition, but had "a right relation to God outside the boundaries of Israel's covenant" (*WGM*, 26). By the way, not all of God's revelatory initiatives related to salvation, though all related to His purposes (e.g., the judgment curse on nature, Cain, Noah's generation, etc.). All these men had a right relation to God *before* the Abrahamic covenant and Israel's covenants were instituted. They came from God's salvific tradition. The early chapters of Genesis portray that before God narrowed his special revelatory scheme to the Jewish nation, that divine *salvific* (along with revelatory) initiatives were undertaken by Him. These initiatives may be considered extraordinary from our perspective but not from the recipient's viewpoint. In that time, direct, existential immediacy with God was seen as something normal with *normative* implications. For example, Noah walked with God (Gen. 6:9), and God gave him His normative revelation of upcoming judgment and the exclusive means of salvation.

The time period of these divine salvific initiatives in the spectrum and history of salvation classifies everyone who was saved as falling under this extraordinary initiative of God—Adam, Eve, Abel, Seth, Enoch, Noah, Melchizedek, Job, Abraham, Isaac, Jacob, and so on. (Again, Abraham himself was from a non-Abrahamite tradition; cf. Deut. 26:5.) Unfortunately, Scripture does not portray masses of humans coming into salvation during that time, which would justify the inclusivist's wider-hope conclusion. The redeemed were really few in number at that time, and those left out of the divine initiatives, that we know about, were incredibly large in number. More often, there were massive judgments rather than massive salvations. The others mentioned as standing under the Melchizedek umbrella were all divinely nudged into contact with Israel, the news-bearers of salvation, as she fulfilled her elective missionary role: Jethro with Moses (Ex. 18:11: "Now I know that the Lord is greater than all the gods"); Balaam (attempts to make contact with the Lord, Num. 22:8); Naaman with Elisha (2 Kings 5:15: "I know there is no God in all the earth, but in Israel"), the Queen of Sheba with Solomon (cf. 2 Chron. 9:8, where she blesses Solomon's God), Nebuchadnezzar with Daniel (Dan. 4:34ff.); Nineveh with Jonah (Jonah 3:5).

Let us examine the Melchizedek case itself. As one of those who had received divine initiatives of revelation and salvation, Melchizedek received Abraham's obeisance and tithes. The narrative suggests that he was already a priest of the true God with very specific revelation and responsibilities for bearing bread and wine. He had at least as much as or more divine revelation than Abraham. Now, why did Abraham regard Melchizedek as superior? Abraham recognized that God's specific revelation to Melchizedek surpassed his own specific revelation from God. Melchizedek blessed Abraham and the God Most High who had intervened on Abraham's behalf. If the point needs to be pressed with reference to our issue, we end up with recipients of special revelation (inclusivism's Judaism and Christianity represented by Abraham) bowing (affirming the rightness of their status with God Most High) to the recipients of other special revelation (represented by Melchizedek).[12] The worse difficulty is that Melchizedek is used by the author of the Hebrews, not to hint at a wider-hope, but to narrow his audience to the unique necessity of the better priest-king, Jesus Christ. The writer uses Melchizedek "to show something of the uniqueness of Christ and something of the greatness of the work he accomplished for humanity."[13]

Abimelech, too, is employed to show that he "had a right relation with God outside the boundaries of Israel's covenant" (*WGM*, 26). But Abimelech, who protested his own and his nation's innocence, had to have the offender Abraham intercede for the multiplication of his posterity. The Abimelech narrative (Gen. 20) allows us to conclude that God had access to his mind through a dream, but it is not necessarily because he had a right relationship with God. (There are other divine revelatory initiatives without salvific content—for example, divinely placed dreams of historical events to Pharaoh, Nebuchadnezzar—that could lead to hardening or salvation.) There was "fear of God" (i.e., fear of retributive consequence) in Abimelech's environment in relation to taking another man's wife, as is true in many cultures today.[14]

The rest of the inclusivist treatment of the Old Testament has to do with verses that point to God's care and control of national histories (e.g., Amos 9:7: Philistine and Aramean Exodus events) or passages from the prophets speaking of salvation or judgment on non-Jewish nations (e.g., Isa. 19:25). There is no dispute about the prophetic hope of future salvation for all who turn to the true God from anywhere in the world. Pinnock's conclusion from the material is that "God is in dialogue with the nations" (*WGM*, 27–29). This seems to be a harmless inference, except he wants to see it in the context of a more extensive *salvific* dialogue with the nations than the Bible permits. For example, he writes about Jonah: "Along these lines, it is clear from the book of Jonah that God cares for the people of Nineveh and wants to save them too. Even though the Assyrians were fierce enemies of Israel and a cruel people, God is prepared to accept their acts of repentance" (*WGM*, 28).

What does the above statement establish except that Jonah had to preach an exclusive truth to the Ninevites? It does not prove the point that inclusivists ultimately want it to—salvifically acceptable acts of repentance outside salvation history. All that the statement confirms is that: "There is no limitation here. Apparently any nation or kingdom on earth can turn from its wickedness and receive divine mercy" (*WGM*, 29). There is no debate here. The pertinent cleavage between exclusivist and inclusivist is on what basis and on whose terms are the issues of salvation and destiny in the Old Testament.

THE NEW TESTAMENT

In this section, we shall look at some inclusivist reasoning from the New Testament. New Testament support for the inclusivist axiom of universal access to salvation is even less convincing than Old Testament support.

The Gospels

Just as Old Testament missiological passages are harnessed, gospel texts in which Jesus focuses on non-Jews or speaks of non-Jewish salvation are cited as support for inclusivist conclusions. But as one looks up each case, the people in question had to come to Jesus. Why did all these non-Jews have to come to Jesus?

Jesus' circumscription of His ministry to the house of Israel certainly poses a formidable problem for the inclusivist (Matt. 10:5; 15:24). But this is handled as confusing "penultimate means with ultimate ends. Although God had a special arrangement with Israel which Jesus had to pursue, the overarching goal was the inclusion of Jew and Gentile in the kingdom of God (Mt 8:11)" (*WGM*, 31). The special arrangement with Israel was a penultimate ("next to the last") means to the ultimate end of inclusivism. Unfortunately for the inclusivist, Jesus' exclusive attention to the house of Israel, though penultimate, cannot be ruled out for even a syllable moment of time. If God is exclusivistic for even a brief time, it questions the inclusivist thesis. Such alternating between exclusivism and inclusivism casts a cloud of arbitrariness on the nature of God and the mission of Jesus. We must ask how ultimate is the penultimate arrangement? And why? If Jesus' mission was circumscribed in any period of history, why would it not be a coherent position to insist on Christ's exclusivity for all people today? As has been seen in the Old Testament, and in Jesus' mission to the lost sheep of Israel, God has always been exclusive. A position that sees Christ as penultimately exclusive but ultimately inclusive does not do justice to Scripture or theology. We simply hold that Jesus as the critical object of Israel's faith and the bringer of salvation (cf. the commission of Matt. 10) has been enlarged to becoming the critical object of the world's faith and bringer of salvation to all nations (cf. the commission of Matt. 28).

The Book of Acts

Paul's Lystra speech is summoned for the inclusivist thesis, but it cuts both ways. Paul says "in the past, God let all nations go their own way" (Acts 14:15–17). What kind of a dialogue did God carry on with the nations (cf. Pinnock's case for the universal salvific will) if He was letting nations go their own way?

The inclusivist treatment of the Athenian speech shows an ambiguity as well: "Paul thought of these people as believers in a certain sense, in a way that could be and should be fulfilled in Jesus Christ" (*WGM*, 32). On this thought, any theist could be a believer "in a certain sense." But Paul continues that this worship of the unknown God does not get the people off the hook on the day God has fixed for judging the world by the resurrected Man who has been appointed—Jesus (Acts 17:31).

The Epistles

Pinnock's opinion on Romans 1–3 is curious: "It is wrong to read into [Paul's] words in Romans the idea that he is denying that many Jews and Gentiles in the past have responded positively to God on the basis of this light, as Luke also intimates in the book of Acts" (*WGM*, 33). Even a cursory examination of Romans 1–3 concludes that all are under sin (3:9); there is not one who seeks for God on his own (3:10–11); and all fall short of bringing God glory (3:23). The book of Romans is not particularly useful for the inclusivist thesis except for some broad interpretive comments controlled by their theological precommitments. Luke's (and Paul's) comments in Acts confirm that in the past the nations went their own way (14:16–17) during times of ignorance (17:30) and did not experience wholesale, large responses to God's light. Also, it may be easy to cite the major *universalistic,* present reconciliation or future subjection passages (Rom. 5:18; 1 Cor. 15:20–28; 2 Cor. 5:18–21; Phil. 2:6–11; Col. 1:16–20), but these are not entirely useful for anyone who is less than a universalist, and inclusivists are not universalists. We cannot but all agree that there is "a dimension of universality" (*WGM*, 34) here as well as in Pauline passages such as 1 Timothy 2:4–6 and 4:10.

Sanders sees Gentile salvation in the New Testament as pointing to universal salvation too. This is to motivate us to include Gentiles in the kingdom. Citing Barnabas Lindars, he writes "the salvation of the Gentiles drove him [Paul] to formulate a distinct theory of universal salvation which really has no precedent" (*NON*, 137). Of course, Paul's theory cannot be a distinct one since Sanders argues for universal salvation in the Old Testament—especially in the coming of non-Jews (Gentiles) to salvation. Either Paul had a distinct theory or not. I hold, instead, that Gentile conversion was not distinct for Paul. There are ample evidences of it in both character and intention in the Old Testament. New Testament distinctness was in co-heirship—that the Gentiles are on par with the Jews in this "body" concept (Eph. 3:1–5). Both Jews and Gentiles had to relate specifically to Christ. (Our final chapter addresses the issue from the perspective of a theology of discontinuity between the Old and New Covenants as a resource to handle some of the issues inclusivists raise with exclusivism.)

The Book of Revelation

John's vision in Revelation is supposed to augment inclusivist reasoning because it shows the wide scope of Christ's work. However, there is no inclusivist point to this statement and to the verses used from Revelation except that the scope of Christ's work was international.

To close out our discussion on the biblical support for the universality axiom of inclusivists, I again object to proving God's universal salvific will from passages where all we find is the plans of God's worldwide heart and their international implementation. These international passages do blast any cultural narrowness that idolatrously fashions election into privilege. But the passages do not counter a "fewness" doctrine of restrictivist salvation with a "manyness" doctrine of inclusivist salvation. When understood in this balanced perspective, the texts undercut the foundation on which the key hypotheses of inclusivism are built.

Are there other means and arguments, in addition to those discussed above, by which heaven is seen as being more heavily populated than the usual evangelical view allows? The answer to that question is yes, and this will be analyzed in the next chapter. But sufficient for us here is the conclusion that the Bible does not prefer either a rigid optimism (cf. massive judgment passages) or a strict pessimism (cf. non-Jewish salvation passages) of salvation. The Bible does promote an awesome responsibility of salvation based on God's universal mercy.

Notes

1. Several missiological textbooks consider the missionary nature of the Old Testament. For instance, see works by George W. Peters, Richard R. De Ridder, Donald Senior and Carroll Stuhlmueller, and Roger E. Hedlund in the Bibliography. The section in Pinnock's book denoted as a "hermeneutic of hopefulness" runs parallel to the treatment of OT missiology in the above books.

2. The same Hebrew words ("calling"—*qara;* and "name"—*shem*) are used in reference to Seth's naming his son as well as persons' calling on YHWH. In this context, "calling" with the prepositioned "name" of YHWH was invocational (Brown, Driver, and Briggs, *Hebrew and English Lexicon of the Old Testament [BDB]* [Oxford: Clarendon, 1977], p. 895, 2c; p. 90, 4) and worshipful (*BDB,* p. 1028, 3).

3. L. J. Coppes, "qara," in R. Laird Harris, G. L. Archer, and B. K. Waltke, eds., *Theological Wordbook of the Old Testament (TWOT),* 2 vols. (Chicago: Moody, 1980), 2:810–11.

4. A relation of this feature to the Old Testament view of religions is in 1 Kings 18:24–26. Elijah challenges Baal's prophets, to "call upon the *name* of your god, and I will call on the *name* of the Lord." The Hinduistic and inclusivistic "nameless essence behind all names" is self-refuting—the "nameless, unnamed one" will be its/his name.

5. W. C. Kaiser, "*shem,*" in *TWOT,* 2:934–35.

6. Special mention could be made here of other passages that carry the "name" theme. For instance in John 1:12, receiving Christ is equated with believing in His name as the condition to the right to become children of God. In Revelation 11:18, reward is given to Almighty God's bondservants, the prophets, and to the saints who fear His *name.* The climax of the *kenosis* passage (Phil. 2) is the bestowment of the "name above every name" on Jesus. Here, "the name of Jesus" relates to God's unmodified, unchangeable will in generating universal obeisance and confession.

7. The phrase may be attributed to Johannes Blauw's treatment of the Babel event (*Missionary Nature of the Church* [New York: McGraw-Hill, 1962]). Inclusivists may reply that the Babel event shows willful rejection of God and thus does not apply to his category. Yet, to read the early chapters of Genesis without the judgment motif at all is highly selective. Judgment falls on those who willfully (cf. Babel) or passively (cf. the audience that was geographically outside Noah's pre-Flood preaching) rejected God. Why does not Pinnock mention the universal flood of Noah's time? The Flood certainly affected those who had not willfully rejected God.

8. *WGM,* 23. The "principle of representation" is good Calvinist doctrine, except that Pinnock applies a Calvinist view of Adam ("Adam stood . . . as

the representative head of the entire human race in the covenant of works" [L. Berkhof, *Systematic Theology* (Grand Rapids: Eerdmans, 1939, 1941), 42]) to Abraham's connection to the race. While Pinnock goes on to say that Calvin dreads the Abrahamic "principle of representation," the "principle of representation" seems to carry a typical, federal (from the Latin *foedus*, "covenant") theology flavor, wherein the head is not just an example but a representative transmitter of choices and effects to posterity.

9. See Donald H. Akenson, *God's Peoples: Covenant and Land in South Africa, Israel and Ulster* (Itaca, N.Y.: Cornell Univ. Press, 1992), for the constructive and destructive impetus that "covenant elitism" encouraged against the "Canaanites" in those lands.

10. Bruce Demarest, *General Revelation: Historical Views and Contemporary Issues* (Grand Rapids: Zondervan, 1982), has a useful phrase "special revelatory initiative," to refer to these kinds of situations. These initiatives are found in "exceptional circumstances" and "extraordinary ways" (p. 260). However, a distinction between "divine revelatory initiatives" and "divine salvific initiatives" would have been helpful, with the rule that all revelatory and salvific initiatives that are consistent with the Scriptures are divine initiatives.

11. Some hold Melchizedek to be a theophany or Christophany—an Old Testament visible manifestation of Christ—in which case he becomes irrelevant to this question (cf. the title "King of righteousness" and Hebrews 7:8, where he is "declared to be living"). Yet, even if he is not the theophanic Christ, it is difficult to verify the inclusivist point from this narrative.

12. An implication for the religions may be drawn. Abraham did not bow to the king of Sodom nor accept anything from him. Certainly, this was an indictment of a non-true religion. Melchizedek was a pre-figure of Christ. Therefore, we must bow to Christ alone.

13. Leon Morris, "Hebrews," in *Expositor's Bible Commentary* (Grand Rapids: Zondervan, 1981), 62.

14. From ethnographic research and cross-cultural readings, I agree with C. S. Lewis, *The Abolition of Man* (New York: Macmillan, 1947), 109, who refers to the law of justice and sexual justice as found universally.

3

HOW PARTICULAR IS GOD'S TRUTH?

Each year I seek to speak to a couple of campus audiences in North America on the truth claims of Christ. An Indian name and a non-North American origin initially gives credibility among some audiences. I have a talk on "Eastern Mind/Western Man: Fission, Fusion, Confusion," which attracts those who normally do not attend "Christian" events. Of course, there is no way I can tell who is of Christian bent or not.

We had an excellent turnout one particular night at a state university. I finished the talk, took questions, and then invited people to come up to continue the dialogue privately.

A young man who had several questions in public was the first to rush forward. He threw my outline on the desk and said: "As long as you were speaking about God you were superb, but once you introduced Jesus Christ as that God you messed up the whole thing."

I saved his notes as a lasting reminder of an austere fact. Jesus Christ as uniquely God is a permanent offense, an infraction of pluralist sensibilities. Once we specify and particularize God to be Jesus Christ, we mess up the world of religion.

Simply speaking, in this chapter I am going to biblically and theologically assess the possibility of separating God from Jesus. As quoted in the preliminary dialogue, the Christological particularity axiom of the inclusivist "consists of the finality of Jesus Christ as the decisive manifestation and ground of God's grace toward sinners" (*WGM*, 49). I have also mentioned that one can find in Pinnock a clear and tight apologetic for a high Christology against the revisionist Christology of liberal theology. However, inclusivists are unwilling to see personal faith in Jesus Christ as the necessary content and condition of God's grace toward sinners. This is done (and has been by others) by placing some distance between God and Jesus. What follows is a critique of the major angles of the inclusivist argument concerning the God-Jesus split.

CHRIST'S UNIQUENESS
AND THE INCARNATION MODEL

According to Pinnock, a biblical theism points to the uniqueness of Israel's God and should be the context for assessing Christology.

> Uniqueness belongs first of all to the God of the Bible; and, if it should be said that Jesus is unique, it will only be because of the special relation to God he is thought to enjoy as God's Son. Uniqueness and finality belong to God. If they belong to Jesus, they belong to him only derivatively. (*WGM*, 53)

It does not take much intellectual effort to see why inclusivists would ascribe only a "derivative" uniqueness to Christ. In this way "God," the source of uniqueness, could be kept distinctly approachable outside Christ, who is only derivedly unique. However, a derivative uniqueness is not particularly complimentary to Christ, nor is it compatible with the biblical data. The word derivative gives a secondary status to Christ, with "uniqueness" not intrinsic or necessary to Him. The source, origin, fountainhead, root, or stem of Christ's uniqueness is someone of higher, primary (at least, temporally so), and independent status, namely, the God of the Bible.

Although reasons for this stratification in the existence and relations in the Christian godhead are consistent within the inclusivist argument, it is not a correct or comprehensive treatment of the biblical material. Evangelicals hold that uniqueness belongs to the God of the Bible and that Jesus is the God of the Bible. Jesus is the YHWH of the Old Testament (cf. Ex. 3:14 and John 8:58); the creator of all things (cf. Gen. 1:1 and John 1:1); and eternal (John 8:58—the Son to be born is to be named "Everlasting Father," Isa. 9:6; cf. also Mic. 5:2 and the other fetal trinitarian passages in the Old Testament). He is not lower than, deficient to, or secondary to, in any ontological sense, the God with whom He shares generic oneness (John 10:31). The gospel of John is especially adamant about His actual uniqueness ("he who has *known* and *seen* me has *known* and *seen* the Father," John 14:7, 9; italics added). Johannine insistence on Jesus' exclusive claims and implications was contrary to a Jewish monotheistic understanding of God and is proved by their adverse reaction to Jesus' declaration (John 10:33). The Jews were clear about Jesus' claiming an identical, not a derived, uniqueness with God. Jesus' bold declaration that "all may honor the Son, even as they honor the Father" does not beg for inferior respect. Indeed, "he who does not honor the Son does not honor the Father who sent him" (5:23; also see v. 24).

I have intentionally drawn many of these texts from the gospel of John, because Pinnock's book does not use the Johannine argument for Christ's unique and exclusive deity. We appreciate his submitting less familiar arguments for a high Christology, but Pinnock does not see John as serving his case. Therefore, if the Johannine model is not integrated into a controlling model of Christology, several of the incarnational passages become insignificant. Pinnock argues that a Johannine "incarnation as a metaphysical fact" was not a necessary development nor do evangelicals need to perpetuate it (*WGM*, 62). A sample of his hesitance in using John may be presented in the following statements. "Theological pluralists feel strongly that in the interests of interreligious peace and harmony we should not do so (that is, perpetuate the incarnation doctrine)" (ibid.). "Incarnation language stands alongside the other modes of interpretation testifying to Jesus as the Savior of the world" (ibid.). "Incarnation is not the normative category for Christology in the New Testament" (ibid.).

I do not concede the conclusion nor the theological method in this all important matter.

First, it is evangelically inconsistent to set up John against the other gospel writers (the synoptics). To see the Incarnation as only a Johannine model—merely one of several models in the Bible—does not make it any the less authoritative. Inasmuch as one gospel writer mentions the Incarnation, it cannot but become a normative category to be included in a credible and comprehensive Christology. Pinnock has to let the whole Bible speak to this issue. (Elsewhere, he desires the whole Bible to speak to an issue. The "narrow path" passage of Matthew 7:14 is dismissed as not keeping with *the whole of Scripture* [*WGM*, 154] in the presence of the other passages. Here is a synoptic verse against inclusivism that is played down.)

Second, there are other biblical writers who are just as clear on Jesus as the enfleshment of God. Paul says Jesus existed in the form of God and had equality with God (Phil. 2:6) but emptied Himself, being made in the likeness of men, being found in appearance as a man (Phil. 2:7–8). Paul also sees Jesus as the incarnation of God's nature and discloses the uniqueness and exclusiveness of God in Jesus as a man, "In him all the fullness of the godhead dwelled in him bodily (Col. 2:9; cf. 1:19, *somatikos,* i.e., "corporeally").[1] If Paul had simply written "fullness," he would have gotten his point across. But in typical Pauline style, he writes "all the fullness." The construction is repetitive and redundant, but is emphatic and exclusive. Also, the writer of the Hebrews declares that the Jesus who tasted death (a "body" feature), being made lower than the angels (2:9), was "the exact representation" of God's nature" (1:3, *hupostasis*).[2]

Third, interreligious peace and harmony are less than decisive criteria for a trustworthy and total Christology. The development of doctrine within the Scriptures cannot be disregarded in developing a theological conclusion. The whole Bible must speak to the issue, even if interreligious peace is threatened. Presently, there are so many amiable and courteous first-generation converts to the Christian faith who have felt the sword of division within their families because of this issue of the exclusive uniqueness of Christ (Matt. 10:34–39). Of course, sacrificing Jesus' exclusivity on the altar of interreligious peace makes a mockery of martyrs who sacrificed their lives for their understanding of this truth over the ages.

Actually, other religions also can subscribe to the kind of Christological uniqueness that inclusivism holds, except with customized substitutions. For example, in discussing the terms *finality* and *particularity* of Jesus, Sanders writes, "Jesus as the Son of God is the highest, clearest, and absolutely normative expression of the character of God" (*NON*, 26). Christians claimed this, until Muslims came by with their substitution. Then, of course, the Bahais claimed the same for their prophet. In the context of world religions, we cannot but proclaim the "absolute, non-derived uniqueness" (Sanders even hesitates to use the term uniqueness in his book) of Christ. Instead of the qualified finality given to Jesus by the inclusivists, I would suggest the following amplification, "Jesus as the Unique Son of God is the only, exact, normative representation of God." Consequently, interreligious peace will be hard to come by with Muslims, Jews, or others if they are first approached on a Christological ground.

Fourth, if Jesus is only derivatively unique, why become a Christian at all? If Jesus was unique because Israel's God was unique, then the unwitting conclusion is that Old Testament Judaism is a valid religious option. This also means that Christians could follow the underived, unique, Jewish God without biblical qualms. Is this Christology high enough?

The Christology of some Christian cults acknowledges such a derived uniqueness to Christ. Gnostic Unitarians (a pluralist and universalist group) and the Arianite Jehovah's Witnesses (an exclusivist group) deny that Jesus was the same substance as God. They too separate Jesus of Nazareth from sharing the eternal deity or the substance of godhood in all its strength. The "derived uniqueness" of Jesus as different from cult versions of derived uniqueness needs to be explicated by Pinnock lest he and other inclusivists, in a sort of guilt by association, be lumped in with the error of the cultists. C. Braaten makes an alert point on this issue. "I maintain that the underlying Christology of the new theocentric pluralists is a new edition of Arianism, in which Christ stands one rung below God on the ladder of being."[3] We must not attempt to dismantle essential intratrinitarian relationships, as inclusivists need to do when referring to uniqueness.

To deal with the Incarnation problem, Pinnock commends the stance of Second Vatican Council: "God's grace is global and that the belief in the Incarnation complements and does not cancel that fact" (*WGM*, 74). There is a major debate about this wider interpretation of the wisdom and spirit of the Council.[4] Suffice it to say here that in the inclusivist interpretation, the Incarnation is not necessary and intrinsic to the structure of God's global (salvific) grace. It is but complementary. A thorough-going Christian pluralism (which Pinnock disavows) could echo the same complementarity opinion about the Incarnation.

In inclusivist theology, there is an emptying of the implications of the uniqueness of the Incarnation. Listen to this sub-evangelical statement on Christ's uniqueness. "But would the uniqueness of Jesus have to mean exclusivity? Not necessarily.

Was not the Buddha a unique religious figure in his own way? There is room in the world for many unique people, even many religious leaders" (*WGM*, 63–64). Pinnock does not deny that there is incompatibility between the two religious leaders but nevertheless affirms complementarity between some of their teachings. Jesus' uniqueness is downplayed to a general uniqueness that may be attributed to any historical personage. Instead, we maintain that the constitutional uniqueness of Jesus directs us to exclusivity in a strong sense. Pinnock would like the word uniqueness but not exclusiveness. Is this possible in Jesus' case—a case of one?

PLURALISM AND A TRINITARIAN REDEMPTION

Pinnock contributes an excellent critique of the "ideology of pluralism" as an incoherent, modern dogma that is not aware or serious about its own beliefs (*WGM*, 69ff. Here follows a summary statement of Pinnock's arguments against pluralism.). He points out the pluralist premise against Christian uniqueness, "It would be unfair for truth not to be equally and simultaneously present to everyone" (*WGM*, 70). However, this "unfairness" premise is part of the reason for inclusivism. Pinnock asks, "Is it fair to exclude them (the millions of unevangelized) without having a chance to be saved?" (*WGM*, 149). "God's universal salvific will implies the equal universal accessibility of salvation for all people" (*WGM*, 157). If he accuses restrictivist evangelicals of unfairness, then he cannot chide pluralists for bringing up the problem in conversation with Christians.

In the section, "Does a High Christology Entail Narrowness?", Pinnock undercuts much of what was said about the uniqueness of Christ in his earlier section (*WGM*, 74ff., especially p. 77). The Logos, who is present throughout world and human history, was made flesh in Jesus of Nazareth. "The second Person of the Trinity was incarnate in Jesus, but is not totally limited to Palestine" (*WGM*, 77). Apparently, the Logos is the second person of the Trinity. This second person of the Trinity is outside and beyond Jesus, for Jesus was physically limited to Palestine. "We need to realize that our insisting that God is embodied and defined by Christ does not mean that God is exhausted by Christ or totally confined to Christ" (ibid.). Pinnock recognizes a pre-Incarnation Logos, the cosmic Christ, as "God's way of more going on by way of redemption than what happened in first-century Palestine" (ibid.), and "the way to confess the Incarnation without it being a hindrance to openness" (*WGM*, 78). He also believes that the Holy Spirit is not "tied to the Christ-event exclusively but rather can operate in the whole world, which is the Father's domain" (ibid.). The "triune God is free to work out the application of his love and salvation for humankind in the ways he chooses" (*WGM*, 79).

We certainly affirm God's freedom to choose the way of redemption. But God can be free(d) to choose a reproachful, narrow way. Also, inclusivists need to posit the second person of the Trinity as beyond and outside the Jesus of Nazareth in Palestine. We agree that there was no Jesus *of Nazareth in Palestine* before the Incarnation. But Jesus of Nazareth in Palestine was the eternal Son. In addition to the verses cited in the text, John 3:16: "gave his one and only son"; 3:17: "did not send his son"; and Romans 8:32: "did not spare his son" cannot be easily interpreted in a way other than looking at Jesus Himself as the Son before the Incarnation. Pinnock finds it difficult to refer to this Palestine-born Jesus as the eternal Son, and thus the second person of the Trinity. (Pinnock believes in the eternal Son. "Sent by God, the eternal Son and Logos upholds all things by his power and enlightens everyone coming into the world" [*WGM*, 103]. He is only hesitant to name Jesus of Nazareth as the eternal Son and vice versa.)

Let us check a few passages that recognize Jesus as the eternal Son and as pre-incarnately active. John 17:24 declares, "The Father loved the Son before the foundation of the world"; he had "glory with the Father before the world" (v. 3). Here, Jesus, born and brought up in Palestine, claims to be the eternal Son. And now because God has spoken finally in His Son (Heb. 1:1–2), we cannot continue to posit the salvific activity of the second person of the Trinity outside and beyond Christ. Was God at any time totally confined to Christ? To answer that question, we would again bring Paul's assertion of all the fullness of the godhead dwelling in Christ bodily. There was nothing of the godhead left to dwell in another thing or person. The localization of deity is exclusively in Jesus. Pinnock does not cite Colossians 2:9, a verse that undermines his point. I agree with Pinnock's affirmation that, as the Lord of history, "God has more going on than what happened in first century Palestine." But I do not agree that this activity presently or necessarily involves eternal salvation. Jesus Himself said that salvation is from the Jews (John 4:22) when He offered Himself as the giver of the eternal water of life (John 4:10) to a non-Jew.

Matthew 11:27 makes an important contribution to incarnational Christology and the inclusivist epistemology (what a person must know) for salvation. Jesus says, "All things have been handed over to Me by my Father; and no one knows the Son, except the Father; nor does anyone know the Father, except the Son, and anyone to whom the Son wills to reveal Him." Jesus says more than Pinnock asserts in "He (Jesus) knew God in a way that only a Son could know him" (*WGM*, 58). Although there is a differentiation of quantity in parent-child relationships—a son may know his father more or less intimately—Jesus here is making a qualitative differentiation. Major metaphysical and salvific implications are evident in this verse for Jesus claims to be *the only one* who knows the Father, so that in relation to a later question of the epistemology of salvation, Jesus follows in the next verse with a universal invitation, "come to me, *all* who are weary" (Matt. 11:28).

A bitter split in church history (the Filioque Controversy) occurred over whether the Spirit proceeded from the Father and the Son (double procession) or just from the Father.[5] "Filioque" means "and from the Son." Pinnock uses the East-West ecclesiastical split (A.D. 1054) over the filioque clause (cf. John 15:26) in the Nicene Creed to conclude that the Spirit's operation outside the Son may be necessary. If the Son is the same substance as the Father, then the filioque clause is legitimate. The issue for us is if the Spirit was operative outside the Son in the Father's revelation and if the post-incarnate salvation activity of the Spirit is commensurate with the Spirit's pre-incarnate salvation activity.

Again, we go to relevant Scriptures. The Son speaks of the Spirit's universal convicting activity when He eventually comes (John 16:8). So, though the Spirit is very active before the Incarnation, there is the Son's special commissioning of the Spirit after the Incarnation.[6] If the Holy Spirit's chief activity as the Spirit of truth is to bear witness of Jesus (John 15:26) and to glorify the Son (John 16:14), then His intentional, pre-evangelistic activity toward salvation gives us encouragement in our missionary endeavors. The filioque issue is not as determinative as Pinnock would like it to be, for the Spirit's commissioning by the Son to the world was yet to come when Jesus spoke the words. And once the commissioning occurs, the post-incarnate salvific activity of the Spirit singularly refers to the Son, as He convicts the world of sin, righteousness, and judgment (John 16:8–11). The Holy Spirit convicts the *world* of sin, because they do not believe in Jesus (John 16:9).

This examination of the salvific activity of the triune God yields an opposite conclusion to "there is no hint of the grace of God being limited to a single thread of human history" (*WGM*, 78). The past arrival of the single thread of God's salvific grace with a universal focus is clear, "The grace of God has appeared bringing salvation to all men (Tit. 2:11)." First Timothy 2 is also clear on this single, historical, connection between God and man. God's wishes are inclusive (v. 4*a*), but God's truth is exclusive (v. 4*b*–6). There is one God, and one mediator between God and men, the man Christ Jesus, who gave Himself as a ransom for all, the testimony at the proper time.

Ontology and Epistemology

A watershed issue between evangelicals[7] and Pinnock now comes to the fore. Can a person be saved apart from specific knowledge of Jesus Christ? Pinnock continues with the commendation of the Second Vatican Council, "The Council knows how to distinguish the ontological necessity of Christ's work of redemption from the epistemological situation of sinners" (*WGM*, 75). Evangelicals may also make such a distinction. The epistemological situation of sinners is dismal because they live(d) in unevangelized areas and times. They do not know of Jesus Christ and His offer of salvation.

However, Pinnock's conclusion to non-Christian epistemological dismalness[8] (the fact that they do not know of Christ) is this: "There is no salvation except through Christ but it is not necessary for everybody to possess a conscious knowledge of Christ in order to benefit from redemption through him" (ibid.). "The Bible does not teach that one must confess the name of Jesus to be saved" (*WGM*, 158). Job, David, and infants who die(d) did not know the name of Jesus. So, the theological problem is more than a distinction between the ontological necessity of Christ's work and the epistemological situation of sinners. The issue is the epistemological necessity of Christ's work for personal salvation. To this pivotal question, we now turn.

Earlier in his book, Pinnock had castigated pluralists because they "hope there is a way to read the New Testament without coming up with a Christ who has to be normative for everybody in the world. They need a way for Jesus to be unique for his followers, but not necessarily for others" (*WGM*, 64). With little or no adjustment, Pinnock can be firmly located in his own description of pluralism. He does hold Jesus to be normative for everybody's salvation (ontology), but not in the same way (epistemology) for others as He is for His followers. Only believers in Jesus have earthly "fullness of life," but people may be saved without knowledge of Jesus. (Along with the Second Council, the purpose of missions is to help people find the fullness of religious life [*WGM*, 76], full strength salvation, and a "clearer revelation of God's love and forgiveness, and the assurance that goes with love and forgiveness" [*WGM*, 131]. Missions is to show how Christ can make a difference in earthly life.) Pinnock reads the New Testament without coming up with a Christ who has to be epistemologically normative for everybody in the world. God, of course, is epistemologically normative for all people.

We shall now proceed to examine the epistemological necessity of Jesus biblically and theologically. Certainly, I agree with the line of names of people who were redeemed without conscious knowledge of Christ in the Old Testament. But whether this is a continuing, universal paradigm for salvation is the issue. Could people be saved today with pre-Messianic/pre-Christian information and without information about Christ? I have earlier contended that Old Testament salvation was not as general or abstract as inclusivists would like it to be. Redemptive content was universally (for all people) and temporally (for that time period in human history) concrete and specific.

The role and content of progressive (incremental) revelation during the epochs (dispensations) of history become cardinal factors in determining a solution. (Chapter 6 in this book deals with this issue more fully.) There is a qualitative change to the content of salvation for all men in each epoch. There were no simultaneously different paths or contents of salvation within a dispensation. Titus 3:4–7 portrays the universality and particularity dimensions of salvation in a straightforward manner. The universality of Christ's incarnation shows God's love for mankind (Tit. 3:4) and salvific grace for all men (Tit. 2:11). This universal, salvific love demonstrates the terms and conditions by which all mankind would come to salvation after the Incarnation. Contrary to Pinnock's assertion that actions of love and justice by non-Christians are faith-responses to God, even deeds done *in righteousness* do not count as a basis for salvation (Tit. 3:5). The specific content of salvation becomes evident, for not only God (v. 4) but Jesus Christ is our Savior (v. 6). It is not possible for mankind, on the present side of the Incarnation, to be saved on the basis of good actions reflecting its faith in God. People cannot be saved without consciously relating to the Lord Jesus Christ as their Savior. Further, those who are saved in this relationship to Jesus are heirs according to the hope of eternal life (v. 7). That is, those who are not saved in this way are not heirs of eternal life.

For inclusivists, a person's location in a particular time of human history is not decisive in relation to the specifics of his salvation. Historical time is at best secondary to a person's salvation. In this way, there can be an undefined faith principle that is continuously salvific throughout history. (Twice, Pinnock favorably claims dispensationalist Charles Ryrie to show the continuity of faith across dispensations, but he does not take into account the discontinuity of the content of faith in that same Ryrie quote. This too is tackled in chapter 6.) This proposal cuts at the core of, need for, and effect of Christ's historical incarnation. As intimated earlier, such an incarnation is not structurally, but only complementarily, necessary for human salvation. We shall later examine the inclusivists' further inference that pre-Messianic information is present in basic form and/or at least strongly implied in all religions of the world and therefore unconditionally accessible to everyone.

"Jesus": The Name Given. The name "Jesus" means savior from sins (Matt. 1:21). Even His own people, the Jews, could not come just by YHWH anymore. Why was it necessary for Nicodemus, a teacher of Israel, to be introduced to Jesus (John 3), unless it is Jesus who saves and not just a YHWH God who saves? In Acts 2:32, the Jews ask, "Brethren, what shall we do?" The answer is given in verse 38: "Repent and let each of you be baptized in the name of Jesus Christ for the forgiveness of sins." This is Luke's own interpretation of Luke 24:47: "repentance for forgiveness of sins should be proclaimed *in His name* [particularity] to all the nations [universality] beginning from Jerusalem" (italics added). Luke and the apostles did not distinguish between ontology and

epistemology to provide salvific ways outside actual belief in Jesus (cf. Acts 3:18–20). The apostles, who had a set of non-negotiable teachings (Acts 2:42; cf. 2 John 9; Jude 3–4), do not agree that "one third of the human race may believe in Yahweh" (*WGM*, 124–25. "But Yahweh lives in the devotion of hundreds of millions of Jews and Christians" [124].) outside of Jesus, the one whom God exalted to grant repentance to Israel and forgiveness of sins (cf. Acts 5:31). Was Paul grieving over Israel's unbelief in God generally, or in Christ particularly (Rom. 9:1–3)? And was his extreme grief related only to the Jews' missing out on full strength salvation during earthly life?

Acts 4:12 adds further specifications to the issue. Pinnock argues that in Acts 4:12, "Peter is referring to messianic salvation including physical healing through Jesus' name. He is not denying premessianic occurrences of God's grace" (*WGM*, 78–79). Elsewhere, he notes that the verse "was not meant to address the eschatological fate of the unevangelized."[9] A reduction of clear meaning and implications is evident in Pinnock's treatment of other passages as well. For example, in "The Destruction of the Finally Impenitent" *Criswell Theological Review* 4 (Spring 1990): 243–59 (71), he argues that in Matthew 25 Jesus does not define the nature of the eternal life or the eternal punishment. Yet the place prepared for the devil and his angels (Matt. 25:41) is the same place into which the devil will be thrown (Rev. 20:10).

For the moment, let's ignore the issue of Christians receiving physical healing in messianic salvation and probe the verse for its implications. Salvation is in Jesus and by Jesus and in no one else. Both prepositions cannot refer to ontological meaning. We must examine this verse for it displays the ontological grounding *and* epistemological means for salvation. That is, salvation is grounded in Jesus' name (ontology); but salvation is also by knowledge of Jesus' name (epistemology).

First, there is no other (Greek *allo*) name of the same kind; and there is no other (*heteron*) name at all.[10] If epistemology is unimportant, why is the Greek form *heteron* used? The distinguishing of the name (of Jesus Christ of Nazareth, v. 10) is very necessary. Beyer's comment on this verse is instructive:

> The idea of "otherness," which occurs in so many forms, is central to the NT as the story of the fulfillment of the promise of God. The

new which has come in Jesus Christ is something quite different from what has preceded, to the degree that *it excludes everything else* as a way of salvation. There is no other God but one, I C.8:4. And there is no other name under heaven given among men whereby they may be saved but the name of Jesus Christ, Ac. 4:12. This is why the message of the Gospel demands decision.[11]

Second, the Greek *onoma to dedomenon* has a participle form with the constricting article and is to be translated "the given name." "The given name" among men and under heaven, makes the "naming" universally and epistemologically necessary. This is not simply an ontologically decisive name in heaven by which God decides who is saved. Just as the unevangelized are among men and under heaven, this is the *given* name among men and under heaven.

Third, the distinction between the ontological and epistemological necessity of Christ must be evaluated on the basis of whether the apostles recognized such a distinction in proclaiming the exclusiveness of Jesus for salvation. Indeed, the translators have difficulty keeping the English translation of the Greek preposition (*en*) uniform. They translate it "in" or "by" because either meaning is appropriate in the context (cf. Acts 4:2, "in [or "by"] Jesus" (*en to Jesou*); 4:7, "in [or "by"] what name" (*en poio onomati*); 4:10, "by [or "in"] the name" (*en to onomati*); and "by [or "in"] this" (*en touto*). The distinction between the ontology and epistemology of Jesus' name for salvation is something that has been created to support a particular conclusion.

However, even if the distinction is legitimate, Acts 4:12 notes that salvation is "in" (*en*) and "by" (*en ho*) Jesus alone. The first prepositional indicator permits the ontological force. But, the latter indicator points to the necessary (*dei*) means or ground (*en*) and content (*ho*) of human salvation. Now whether the phrase shows the necessary ground or necessary means of salvation, it also shows the necessary content of salvation. Therefore, not only did the apostle not make a distinction between the ontology and epistemology of salvation, he went beyond the ontology of salvation to include the epistemology. The leaders (v. 8), all Israelites (v. 10), and all humans (v. 12), faced the *epistemological* issue of Jesus' name (cf. "made known," v. 10). Salvation is not only grounded in Jesus, but is the name by which anybody "under heaven and among men" may be saved.

The lexical comment on the phrase is epistemologically clear. "The *en onomati* of God or Jesus means in the great majority of cases 'with mention of the name, while naming or calling on the name.' In many passages it seems to be a formula."[12] There is no salvation without actual mention of the name. For instance, I observe as a corresponding note, the epistemological content of the salvific answer to the Jews in Acts 2:38, "have yourself baptized while naming the name of Jesus Christ." (Interestingly, apostolic "name-theology" has a reverse force as well. Could we imagine the demons, who are subject to the name of Jesus, as being only ontologically but not epistemologically subject to Him? His name had to be named for salvation and deliverance.)

Fourth, judgment is implied in the picture for those who are not saved. The rejected stone (Acts 4:11) has a "non-saved" side even if some are saved by it (4:12). What happens to those who are not saved? The word salvation is accompanied by the definite article in the Greek (*he soteria*), for this is *the* salvation Israel was looking for. However, it was not only a physical and earthly salvation, but it was also the means of spiritual and eschatological salvation.[13]

Fifth, Pinnock simply does not do justice to the necessity issue. The Greek word *dei* does not relate how men "may" be saved, but how they "must" be saved. "It is not 'may,' but '*must* be saved,' if saved at all, in this only way."[14]

Sixth, theologically to widen the means of human salvation to more than "this given name" has implications for the nature of God as unity. K. Cragg clarifies concerning "the one 'given name'—'given under heaven', i.e., of and from God in human actuality. Peter is linking the singularity of Christ's redemption with the unity of God."[15] To permit another way of salvation (epistemologically), even though there is only one name (ontologically) introduces confusion in the nature of the One who has given the name by which humanity must be saved.

The Cornelius Factor[16]

We now come to Cornelius as an important factor in this discussion of epistemology, ontology, and eternal salvation. Pinnock points to Cornelius as the pagan saint par excellence of the New Testament, "a believer in God before he became a Christian" (*WGM*, 165).

However, the story may also be used to overturn the inclusivist representation. The narrative really insists that a believer in God *must* become a believer in Christ. Even if one admits that Cornelius was a "God-fearing believer" (*WGM*, 95), he was not a "believer" in Jesus at that time and had to become one. In the progress of the argument of the book of Acts, Jesus becomes epistemologically, and therefore, salvifically critical, to all Jews (Acts 4:1–11), to all Gentiles who had turned to the Jewish God (Cornelius, Acts 10:2, 22; cf. Heb. 11:6 and Old Testament saints), and later to all Gentiles (for example, Acts 16:31). There is the Jesus-condition for salvation for Jew (apostolic sermons in early Acts) and Gentile (apostolic sermons in later Acts). This condition of salvation is proof of the universality and internationality of Jesus Christ and His mission (Acts 1:8). For example, in Acts 13:46–47, Paul saw his personal fulfillment of the vocational election of the Jews, namely, to be a light to the Gentiles to the ends of the earth. In Acts 14:27, Paul reports on how "the door of faith" was opened to the Gentiles. In Acts 15:1–17, the church could be incorporated only with those Gentiles and Jews who bore Christ's name (cf. v. 14)

In Acts 10, Cornelius is loftily described as a God-fearer, alms giver, one who prayed continually, devout and righteous, and given angelic direction. Peter refers to him as one who did what was right. From God's view, he was remembered (cf. 10:4, 31). Now, if this paragon of paganness had to be directed to Christ in this life, why should not everyone else who seeks the true God?

Inclusivists need Peter's conclusive phrase "is welcome" (Acts 10:35) to refer to Cornelius's prior salvific acceptance by God. "Peter is saying that those like Cornelius who have faith in God, wherever they may live in the whole world, are accepted by God in the way Abraham was accepted, on the basis of faith" (*WGM*, 96). However, the point of the verse and the narrative is not to establish God's acceptance of a Gentile independent of and prior to Christ. It is instead to contrast between Peter's religiously-justified bias and God's favorableness to anyone seeking for Him. Jesus' international salvation was exactly opposite of what Peter and the Jews thought. *Dektos* (tr. "welcome," or "acceptable") is not used in the sense of salvation but of non-discriminatory acceptability.[17] People everywhere are welcome to God to be accepted by Him. The verse does not read "welcomed or accepted by Him." It refers to the international availability of salvation and acceptability to God regardless of ethnic origin. It does not speak about a universal accessibility to salvation on people's own religious terms.

The wonderful story of Cornelius cannot be interpreted in a normative way without delving into the Petrine commentary on the salvific admission of this God-fearing Gentile. Otherwise, such an interpretive approach would only offer anecdotal support for a particular position. Peter's sermon continues at least until verse 43. One cannot take the introduction and leave out the rest of the sermon! Peter goes on to refer to Jesus as the One appointed by God to judge the living and *the dead* (v. 42), that *through his name everyone* who *believes in him receives forgiveness* of sins (v. 43). We need to think through the italicized words in the preceding sentence.

If Cornelius's salvation prior to his coming to Jesus could be demonstrated, then it would be support for the inclusivist interpretation. But then, inclusivists would have to explain why Cornelius had to hear of Jesus. According to Pinnock, Cornelius had to be evangelized to give him full-strength salvation on this earth. This interpretation also implies that Old Testament saints, in whose tradition Cornelius supposedly stands, did not have a full-life salvation on this earth because they had not heard of Jesus. Just the thanksgiving and praise Psalms will put that implication to rest. (For Sanders too, "believers in God" have salvation in the present and will receive "salvation in its fullness" in a post-mortem encounter [*NON*, 264]. Christian salvation is distinctly for this life, "Again, this does not diminish the importance of the Christian message of Jesus. We need the message of Christ (salvation in its fullness) to help free us from the ambiguities and futilities of this present life" [238].)

For inclusivists, evangelism is supposed to give a "clearer revelation" and "assurance" of God's love and forgiveness (*WGM*, 179). But verse 43 does not state that belief in Jesus gives a clearer revelation of forgiveness, but the actual reception of forgiveness. Forgiveness of sins is contingent on belief in Jesus.

Also, verse 42 asserts that Jesus has an impact on the next life. He is the Judge of both the living and the dead. Somehow the forgiveness of sins (v. 43) relates to how men relate to Jesus the Judge (v. 42). To escape Christ's post-mortem judgment, one must receive forgiveness of sins through Him by believing in His name in this life. Why should the next-life impact of Jesus be pointed out by Peter, if Cornelius was already a possessor of eternal life without Jesus?

So, Cornelius was not saved before and independent of his encounter with Christ. God remembered him (v. 31) and his righteous deeds and prayers (10:4). In the consistent testimony of the Scriptures, God rewarded this seeker with the knowledge of Christ and His salvation (Heb. 11:6; cf. Jer. 29:13, the injunction to seek God and the promise of finding him to Jews in captivity).

In Acts 10:43 we have two specific phrases relating to the ontology/epistemology question. "Through his name" could possibly refer only to the ontological aspect of salvation. However, "everyone who believes in him" cannot escape the epistemological obligation. "Everyone" (no one excluded) receives forgiveness of sins by this means and in this manner. Putting verses 35 and 43 together, we have the Cornelius paradigm: "in every nation the man who fears God and does what is right is acceptable to Him. When he believes in Jesus he receives forgiveness of sins and is accepted by God." (Regrettably, Acts 10:43 is not mentioned by Pinnock. Consequently, Pinnock is able to see Acts 10:35 as the criteria by which holy pagans are recognized, "one cognitive ['one who fears God'] and ethical ['one who does what is right']" [*WGM*, 96].)

As mentioned earlier, the story actually disproves inclusivist claims for Cornelius. He already worshiped the true God, for he had strong contact with the Jews (v. 22) and even referred to deity as God and Lord (v. 33). But all this was not adequate. In Acts 10:25–26, Cornelius fell at Peter's feet and worshiped him. Peter's report on Cornelius's report of the vision was that Peter would speak words to him by which he and his household would be saved (11:14). Cornelius was not saved until then. Luke's structure of Acts gives further support for this conclusion. The reception of the Spirit by Cornelius the Gentile god-fearer (Acts 10) is parallel to the reception of the Spirit in Acts 2, "for the Holy Spirit fell on them just as He did upon us at the beginning" (11:15). Peter notes that "God gave to them the same gift as He gave to us *after* believing in the Lord Jesus Christ" (11:17, italics added). This gift was the Holy Spirit, which was an incontestable proof of salvation. "God had granted to the Gentiles repentance that leads to life" (11:18). Cornelius had no "life" until then. Like the Jews, he had faith in God but no relationship to Christ, about whom he had to hear (10:36ff.).

I propose a minimum of two conclusions from Peter's interpretation of the Cornelius story for the issue at hand. First, instead of a universal salvific will, Peter submits a universal salvific welcome to anyone from any nation. Second, there is also a particularity axiom—the reception of forgiveness for everyone is through Jesus' name by belief in Him. God rejects no one on the basis of nationality. The Jews wrongly thought they were "acceptable to Him" (and possibly, "accepted by Him") on the basis of national preference. Now men from every nation were acceptable to Him and would be accepted by Him as they related to Jesus. Again, this divine acceptance is seen in the gift of the Holy Spirit that is given without ethnic partiality. Peter then did not refuse baptism to the Gentile believer in Christ. Inclusivists need to give more weight to Peter's conclusions from the Cornelius event, rather than reading the narrative through their prior conclusions.

It is also interesting that Acts 8 (which precedes Cornelius and indicates part of the epistemological pattern of Acts) narrates the story of an important person whom Pinnock does not mention. Why did the Nubian-Ethiopian eunuch have to go to Jerusalem to worship? Here was a worshiper of YHWH who was not a complete proselyte and was actually left out of the provisions of the Law (Deut. 23:1) but not out of millennial blessing (Isa.56:3ff). Though he was already reading Isaiah 53:7, the good news of Jesus had to be told through Philip the evangelist (vv. 34–35). The Ethiopian believed, took baptism, and went rejoicing (v. 39).

No Other Name! One Other Way!

We must now take another look at the inclusivist concept of saving faith. An abstract faith principle without the content or object of Christ's name is considered salvific in all places and times. For the inclusivist, this faith principle becomes the critical negotiating link between the ontology and epistemology of salvation. In this salvific scheme, there is no other name, but there is one other way to salvation.

How is salvation effected? The God of theistic, Judeo-Christian religion is a meta-religious truth that is beyond and above the objective religions that exist. A faith-oriented "heart response" toward this "meta-truth" effects salvation.

According to the inclusivist, this archetypal or transcendent model of theism is manifestly seen in Israel and the Christian faith.

But the theism is only a relative, quantitative advantage for the Israelite and the Christian. A basic salvific element is present in all religions, or at least, to all people. There is no absolute, qualitative difference in the Christian faith pertaining to eternal destiny. As mentioned earlier, this view ends up with no theological necessity for Jesus Christ to have come at all. Of course, special revelation could have progressed or regressed and it would not really have mattered—a faith response to the archetypal theism would have been adequate. We saw earlier that a derivative uniqueness of Jesus builds a case for Old Testament Judaism as a conversion option for non-Christians. Here, I maintain that acquiescing to an unspecified content of faith in the Old Testament yields Old Testament Judaism as a conversion option for everyone, theoretically including Christians as well.

The problem with the faith-principle is its attempt to find a universal core truth—the God (of Judeo-Christian theism) who becomes the object of sincere faith. How the Judeo-Christian God is smuggled in as the object of the faith of the sincere is hard to see. The inclusivist's faith-principle simply does not take into account the radically differing doctrines of God in the various religions, including the monotheistic ones. The major difficulties of the monotheistic religions' coming to terms with Jesus are not just historical (the Holocaust against the Jews or the Crusades against Muslims) but fundamentally theological. For instance, the trinitarianism of the Christian faith and the concentrated monotheism of Judaism are incompatible. Pinnock does have some critical questions for Jews (*WGM*, 143). But it is not at all surprising that he believes Jews and Christians worship the same God. "Yahweh lives in the devotion of hundreds of millions of Jews and Christians" (*WGM*, 124). Only Jews and Christians do not concur with that statement. For instance, Poliakoff notes, "By nature the thoroughgoing monotheism of Judaism cannot embrace trinitarianism."[18] Or consider this outburst, "Judaism is Judaism because it rejects Christianity and Christianity is Christianity because it rejects Judaism."[19]

The faith-principle of the inclusivist really compromises theological incompatibilities between the various religions. Christianity stands against the monotheistic religions of Islam and Judaism with its trinitarianism. It stands against the pantheistic religions with theistic distance. It stands against the deistic religions with the historical Incarnation. So, to find a universal, meta-religious, theistic core as the object of salvific faith is to deface the Christian God. And to find the Judeo-Christian God as the universal, meta-religious core is to defame the non-Christian faiths.

I have already noted that the Old Testament did not have an undefined faith-principle outside YHWH. There can be no unspeci-fied faith-principle in the New Testament either. Both Abraham and Cornelius had divinely revealed, specific content to believe in. The New Testament theology of "belief" stipulates the content of faith. Faith without an object may be sincere but it is empty, invalid, and weak.

It is this stipulated, objective content to saving faith that Paul elaborates in response to the Philippian jailer's question, "Believe in the Lord Jesus and you shall be saved and your household" (Acts 16:31). This believing in the Lord Jesus is equated with hav-ing "believed in God" (v. 34). The faith-principle of the New Testa-ment is believing in Jesus, which is really believing in God.[20]

This equation of belief in God and belief in Jesus is but a reflection of Jesus' own teaching on the subject. In John 14:1–3, Jesus conveys an assuring invitation, "Believe in God, believe also in me." Those who believe in God must believe also in Jesus. The objective content of their belief is exact in phraseology and con-struction. Indeed, Jesus was not only claiming deity and represen-tation, but the lack of differentiation between God and Him. We find the same Jesus-Father sentiment in John 14:10–11: "I am in the Father, and the Father is in Me." We may accede that these disciples already had the faith-principle toward the Father. But they still had to believe in Jesus. And they had to believe in Jesus, not for fullness of earthly life, but for the genuine obtaining of eternal life. These early words of John 14 completely counter the hypoth-eses of soteriological inclusivism. There is no faith-principle out-side belief in Jesus—and it is for heavenly life.

It is difficult to avoid mentioning John 14:6 in this setting of the universality and particularity of Jesus. Jesus claims to be "the way [means], the truth [object], and the life [effect]." He declares that He provides the only link and access for *all* people to the Fa-ther. There is no other way at all. Jesus does not say, "anyone who is saved, is saved by me (ontology); and anyone can come to God in faith, but does not need to come through me (epistemology)." Instead, He asserts that no one (not "no Christian or Westerner") *comes* to the Father, except through me." How does one come to the Father? He comes through the person of Jesus Christ. But His definitive uniqueness also relates to the method of coming to the Father. In the context of this passage, people may come to the Father by believing in Jesus (at least for His works' sake, John 14:11), even as they believe in God. This is an epistemologically conclusive statement for salvation. Jesus not only provides the narrow way to God in salvation, but in the context that follows (vv. 12ff) He shows how people may come to God in prayer. This too reduces the effectiveness of Pinnock's later propositions of "subjective religion" being more important than objective, theological content.

The explicitness of the faith-in-Christ principle is also argued by Paul. Pinnock does not treat the key passages of Acts 16:31 and Romans 10:9–17 in his book. The passages are uncompromising as to the content of faith for salvation. (Romans 10:18 is used by him toward the efficacy of general revelation.) Romans 10:9–17 has a powerful argument about the uniqueness, exclusiveness, sufficiency, and necessity of precise knowledge of Christ for international salvation. First, the summary statement of the passage announces that faith only comes from hearing. There is no faith-principle without hearing. And hearing is by the word of Christ. The word of Christ is the word of faith they are preaching (v. 8). Second, the word of faith they are preaching is the oral confession of Jesus as Lord and the heart belief that God has raised Him from the dead. This results in salvation (vv. 9–10). Third, "whoever" is saved is saved in the same way. There is no distinction between Jew and Greek as far as the condition of salvation; or of the rich, saving Lordship of Christ; or of the means of salvation. Everyone has to believe in Him (v. 11) and/or call on the name of the Lord Christ (vv. 11–13). We cannot escape the Pauline parallelism of Jesus as Lord (v. 9) and the name of the Lord (YHWH, v. 13). Paul's argument is categorically obvious concerning the impossibility of salvation without precise themes. It is impossible to be saved, if people do not call on the name of the Lord (v. 13; i.e., Jesus, from v. 9). It is impossible to call upon Him in whom they have not believed (v. 14a). It is impossible to believe in Him of whom they have not heard (v. 14b). These impossibilities are exactly opposite of what inclusivists are proposing. For Paul, it is impossible to call on the true God without believing in Jesus.

The preceding section confirms that God's concern is not only with the direction of the heart, but also with the content of theology. This is antithetical to Pinnock's statement, "The issue God cares about is the direction of the heart, not the content of theology" (*WGM*, 158). We can neither separate God from Jesus nor the grounds of our salvation from the content of our faith. Ontology and epistemology are indivisibly wedded in Christ's international offering of salvation.[21] God's merciful welcome is universal. God's particular truth is exclusive.

Notes

1. "Bodily" (*somatikos*), "corporeally," Bauer, Arndt, and Gingrich, *Greek-English Lexicon of the New Testament and Other Early Christian Literature (BAG)* (Chicago: Univ. of Chicago, 1957), 807.

2. "Nature" (*hupostasis*) meaning: substantial nature, essence, actual being, reality; *BAG*, 854.

3. C. Braaten, *No Other Gospel!: Christianity Among the World's Religions* (Minneapolis: Fortress, 1992), 21. Braaten also shows neo-gnostic, docetic, and ebionite tendencies in pluralist Christology. These play down the corporeality and humanity or the pre-existence and divinity of Christ.

4. Mikka Ruokanen, *The Catholic Doctrine of Non-Christian Religions According to the Second Vatican Council* (Leiden: E. J. Brill, 1992), effectively argues that "the common interpretation of the Council documents as recognizing non-Christian religions to be capable of specific mediation of God's saving grace is invalid" (116).

5. For introductions to the problem, see H. E. W. Turner, "Filioque," in *The Westminster Dictionary of Theology*, eds. Alan Richardson and John Bowden (Philadelphia: Westminster, 1983), 212; and G. W. Bromiley, "Filioque," in *Evangelical Dictionary of Theology*, ed. Walter A. Elwell (Grand Rapids: Baker, 1984), 415.

6. We are able to establish that both Eastern and Western views would agree on the procession of the Spirit from the Father, and that the commissioning of the Spirit is from Father and Son (i.e., the Son sends the Spirit, John 15:26). If the Spirit's commission by the Son is viewed as a procession issue, then the Spirit proceeds from Father and Son. It helps to notice that the Son is the Spirit of Christ (Rom. 8:9; Gal. 4:6; cf. trinitarian interpretation of Rev. 19:10, "for the testimony of Jesus is the s(S)pirit of prophecy"). See also G. W. Bromiley, "Filioque," in *Baker's Dictionary of Theology* (Grand Rapids: Baker, 1960), 220.

7. It is hard to delimit evangelicalism, especially in the West. For instance, Rowland Croucher senses the burden of the word in the English-speaking world in *Recent Trends Among Evangelicals* (Sutherland, Australia: Albatross Books, 1986), chap. 1. But by any count, Pinnock's thesis is definitely sub-evangelical. It is rather difficult to consider anyone an "evangelical" if he does not emphasize the epistemological necessity of Jesus for salvation, because evangelicalism has always maintained that personal *faith in Christ* is necessary for salvation. R. V. Pierard's article on

evangelicalism includes the following: "Evangelicals believe that salvation is an act of unmerited divine grace received *through faith in Christ*" ("Evangelicalism," in *Evangelical Dictionary of Theology,* ed. Walter A. Elwell [Grand Rapids: Baker, 1984], 379–80). My main criticisms surround the fact that Pinnock wants to be known as an "evangelical." If he gave up his evangelical badge, there would be no argument.

8. It is ironic that those who give major epistemic ability to non-Christians in the areas of faith and reason see a limiting factor in the geographical inaccessibility to the gospel (cf. Pinnock), whereas others who discount geographical distance from the gospel as a limitation have a heightened view of non-Christian epistemic ability to find God (cf. R. C. Sproul, *Objections Answered* [Glendale, Calif.: Regal, 1978], 58).

9. From "Acts 4:12—No Other Name Under Heaven" (110), in William V. Crockett and James G. Sigountos, eds. *Through No Fault of Their Own: The Fate of Those Who Have Never Heard* (Grand Rapids: Baker, 1991), 107–15.

10. "In Acts 4:12, the point of *heteron* is rather that no other name at all than that of Jesus, not that of difference in kind" (A. T. Robertson, *A Grammar of the Greek New Testament in the Light of Historical Research* [Nashville: Broadman, 1934], 749).

11. Beyer, "heteros," in Kittel and Bromiley, *Theological Dictionary of the New Testament* (*TDNT*). 10 vols. (Grand Rapids: Eerdmans, 1967), 2:703 (italics added).

12. *BAG*, 576.

13. The salvation here is more than physical. "'Sozo' is often used with reference to the healing of the sick, though always in the Synoptists, apart from Ac. 4:9, where this verb—followed up in v. 10 by *hugies*—is perhaps chosen because of soteria in v. 12" ("sozo," *TDNT,* 7:990).

14. David Brown, in Robert Jamieson, A. R. Fausset and David Brown, *A Commentary: Critical, Experimental and Practical on the Old and New Testaments* (Grand Rapids: Eerdmans, 1978 reprint), 3:2:23.

15. Kenneth Cragg, *The Christ and the Faiths* (Philadelphia: Westminster, 1986), 225. (See Cragg's fine discussion on Acts 4:12, pp. 224ff.) Later in his interaction with Buddhism, he notes: "'The Name' is not some abstract formula, devised to satisfy a scheme or supply a password. It is the reality of what love means and how it saves and to what it calls in a world we can intelligibly call God's and recognize with honest shame as ours" (278).

16. We wish Don Richardson had gone on in his book, *Eternity in Their Hearts* (Ventura, Calif.: Regal, 1981), to deal with the Cornelius factor to save him from being used for inclusivist purposes. What Richardson meant to portray as only redemptive analogies or pointers divinely built into the languages and cultures of the world is given salvific force by Pinnock. See also, Tite Tienou, "Eternity in Their Hearts?," in Crockett and Sigountos, 209–15.

17. Usage of *dektos* in the New Testament includes human welcoming of prophets, Luke 4:24; "only here of human recognition, elsewhere always of acceptance by God" ("dektos," *BAG,* 173). That God is the referent of

the word is seen Acts 10:35 (a dative of reference?). The word is used of sacrifices (Phil. 4:18); of the favorable (2 Cor. 6:2) *kairos* (cf. "year," Luke 4:19). In these other New Testament occurrences of the word, it is not used in the sense of "acceptedness," or of a past-tense happening.

18. Michael B. Poliakoff, review of *Believing Today: Jew and Christian in Conversation,* by Leon Klenicki and Richard John Neuhaus (Grand Rapids: Eerdmans, 1989), *Journal of the Evangelical Theological Society,* 35 (March 1992): 123.

19. Eliezer Berkowits, in E. F. Talmage, ed., *Disputation and Dialogue: Readings in Jewish/Christian Encounter* (New York: Ktav, 1975), 291 and 293. (Cited by Cragg, 159.) Berkowits sees Judaism as totally self-sufficient and the notion of a Judeo-Christian tradition as fantasy.

20. Sanders's scheme for salvation is similar to Pinnock's, "the unevangelized are saved or lost on the basis of their commitment, or lack thereof, to the God who saves through the work of Jesus" (*NON*, 215). Or, "Saving faith involves the process of moving from some truths about God's character to a degree of trust in the person of God that results in obedience to his will" (228). To a present jailer's question, "What must I do to be saved?" Sanders would answer, "Believe on the God who saves through the work of Jesus (the need for trust in Jesus is inconsequential or at least irrelevant) and you shall be saved."

21. Passages in which Pinnock emphasizes universality but not the epistemological particularity of salvation include:

    2 Peter 3:9: God is not wanting anyone to perish, but that all come to "repentance." God's universal wish does not compromise His exclusive terms. What and for whom is this repentance about?

    1 Tim. 2:5: "God desires all men to be saved and to come to the knowledge of the truth." What and for whom is the truth about? Notice this is the truth that must be preached and taught to the Gentiles (v. 7).

4

WORLD RELIGIONS AND GOD'S UNIVERSAL MERCY: IMPLICATIONS OF A THEOLOGY OF EXCLUSIVISM

In 1993, approximately 7,000 representatives from more than 125 of the world's religions came to attend the second World Parliament of Religions in Chicago. They came a century after the first Parliament of 1893, which represented 41 denominations and religious traditions. Everyone at the commemoration agreed on simple adherence to the Golden Rule: "We must treat others as we wish others to treat us." Lectures and workshops, meditation sessions and ritual dances highlighted the program. A hundred prominent leaders from about a dozen creeds discussed, created, signed, and released a nine-page "Declaration of a Global Ethic." It was a common outline between the faiths decrying environmental destruction, sexual abuse, religious violence, exploitation, genocide, and the like. Its signers pronounced the declaration a historic document, on a par with the Universal Declaration of Human Rights.

A most arresting news item showed a not-so-subtle sign of problems at the Parliament. The story sets the context for our discussion of world religions. Incredibly, the word "God" had to be left out of the 5,000-word "Declaration of a Global Ethic." Why? To include the word God would have "excluded all Buddhists and many faith groups with different views of God and the divine."¹ Another correspondent reported "that writers intended not to exclude any religions that do not recognize one supreme being."[2] In gracious deference to religions that do not include a personal God concept, but recognize a spiritual dimension, they dropped the word God, "coming closest in one reference to 'Ultimate Reality.'"[3] In the opening anecdote of the last chapter, "Jesus" was the offense; "God" was acceptable. At the Parliament of World Religions, "God" was the offense; "Ultimate Reality" was passable. The move by the architects of the global ethic was most convenient and very honest. The move also has major implications for our discussion of world religions and God's wide mercy.

Having considered some of the biblical and theological underpinnings of the inclusivist hypothesis, I now want to deal with the distinctives of its theology of religions. In a significant sense, "a theology of religions" is the parent doctrine of the critical question of the destiny of the unevangelized. Because the ontological and epistemological uniqueness of Jesus Christ ("the grandparent doctrine") is reinterpreted by the inclusivist, some major modifications of an evangelical view of the content, extent, and saving power of truth in world religions are required. How will inclusivists negotiate God and the religions of the world? Will they be honest to a Christian view of world religions? More important, will they be honest to non-Christian views of world religions and the Christian religion?

We make three serious inquiries in this chapter. First, how open should we be to the validity of religious experience in non-Christian religions? Second, to what extent are religions being transformed by Christ so as to enable Christian dialogue with them? And third, what are the implications of God's salvific generosity for the issues of universal access, Christian missions, and the eternal destiny of the unevangelized?

THE STATUS OF
PRESENT RELIGIOUS EXPERIENCE

"Conservatives" judge world religions as false, being "so positive about the religiosity of Christians and so negative about the religiosity of everybody else" (*WGM*, 83). Instead, the inclusivist "couples the church's confession of Jesus Christ with genuine openness to the truth and the goodness found in other religions" (ibid.). How does he go about this genuine openness?

Subjective and Objective Religion

To begin with, inclusivists make a strategic distinction between "subjective" and "objective" religion.[4] Subjective religion has to do with existential faith, piety, and heart response to God, and objective religion refers to institutionalized, cumulative traditions such as Christianity and Buddhism (*WGM*, 84).

This helpful and necessary distinction between objective and subjective religion is often devised by students of world religions. As a descriptive rather than a prescriptive distinction, it has merit. However, adherents of world religions do not necessarily make this distinction about their own (or other) religions. They see their "objective" religion as true, and their "subjective" responses as valid and real responses to their truth. In a broad sense all religious traditions are exclusivist, inasmuch as they maintain their own central affirmations to be true. "So Christian exclusivism is by no means an oddity when considered in the broader context of the global religious traditions."[5] Inclusivists would reply that this exclusivist obstacle is precisely the reason one needs to emphasize the distinction between objective and subjective religion. However, shifting the focus from objective content to subjective faith will not alleviate the question of truth "for we would still have individuals who accept and propagate certain beliefs, dogmas, and teachings, all presumably accepted by believers as true."[6] A case in point is the creedal attempt by a Hindu philosopher to articulate his religious beliefs for the West.[7] Actually, practical experience in cross-cultural apologetics confirms a twofold classification of religions as those which are objectively exclusive *and* those which are *existentially* restrictive. Cragg notes that a most inclusive religion becomes rather restrictive when one of its members converts to another religion.

> The exclusive principle has long been assumed on all hands. Even Hinduism which with some justice prides itself on a hospitable stance is, from that angle, just as rejectionist of Semitic instincts as it sees them to be. An indiscriminating tolerance repudiates intolerance and, so doing, rejects intolerantly faiths whose loyalty requires them to discriminate. It is hard to say which is the more lethal to the other. Hinduism, too, has often showed its resistance to criticism of the caste system and by its very reverence for all reverence can be very irreverent about the will to convert out of it.[8]

Inclusivists also need to distinguish between "religion" and "culture" in order to apply the subjective-objective dimensions of religion in a salvifically optimistic way. "Not that the religious sphere is necessarily the chief sphere in which God approaches human beings. . . . God often gets through to people in the course of secular life" (*WGM*, 108). Yet, this neat division does not account for the pervasive nature of religion in most non-Christian environments. Many religious worldviews are not merely theoretical in nature, they are pre-theoretical solutions to ultimate questions of total reality. Even as we do not spend as much as a second thought in considering the validity of our sense of sight, or even the presence of a window as we admire a sunset, religions are uncritically assumed as there, and true, in people's outlook on the world. So, for the true God to be active outside religion and yet inside culture, is to foist convenient categories that only scholarly observers make and understand.

To imply that subjective "heart responses" (*WGM*, 84–85) to the true God may demonstrate saving faith in the context of contradictory religions, each claiming ultimacy, is naive, reductionistic, or blind.[9] Inclusivists do recognize that the objective sets the framework for the subjective experience. Pinnock writes,

> Of course, the distinction between the subjective and objective dimensions of religion should not be taken so far as to suggest that theology does not matter at all, as if one could ignore objective religion altogether and concentrate entirely on the subjective aspect. This would be ill-advised because religion as a framework and tradition influences religion as faith and trust. It would be wrong to drive a wedge between them. They cannot be kept entirely separate. (*WGM*, 112)

In spite of inclusivist awareness of religious tendency, we shall soon notice that they do end up driving a wedge between the objective and the subjective so that they might facilitate their case for salvation of religious people in non-Christian religions. And, on a scale of emphasis, the objective content of religion becomes rather insignificant. Inclusivists make salvation available on the basis of subjective faith to those who hold frameworks and beliefs that are objectively incompatible with the Christian faith.

For instance, by illustrating from the encounter of Jesus with the Samaritan woman, Pinnock observes that religion in the subjective sense is the Bible's main concern (*WGM*, 85). Jesus recognized her uniqueness as a real person at the level of her heart needs when He offered her living water. Although this is true at the level of her heart need, look at what is overlooked in the argument. The Samaritan woman, a half- or non-Jew, needed to *know* the gift of God and *who it is* who was speaking to her (John 4:9). She needed to drink of the water that *Jesus* gives (vv. 13–14). Jesus emphasized that salvation is from the Jews, dismissed Samaritan claims, and diminished Jewish worship, "when the hour comes and now is" (vv. 21–23a). Her need was subjective; but the religious solution had a concretely objective component, "I who speak to you am He" (v. 26). Jesus beautifully joined the subjective and objective when he made a statement about *true* worshipers (v. 23). True worshipers worship in spirit (subjective relation to the God who is Spirit, v. 24) *and* in truth (objectively discerned, for how else could claims of true and false worship and worshipers be distinguished?). The Samaritans had spirit but not truth; the Jews had truth but not spirit. The Father seeks worshipers in spirit and truth.

Also, John 4 does not portray the Samaritan woman as seeking God, in contrast to Nicodemus (John 3) who sought Jesus by night. This feature is interesting in view of Pinnock's later note, "We must not conclude, just because we know a person to be a Buddhist, that his or her heart is not seeking God" (*WGM*, 112). The problem is that, although Pinnock holds to a "holy pagan" tradition, there is ample verification of a "happy pagan" tradition concerning those who fill their lives with substitute gods and do not even know they are searching. The Samaritan woman would be an example of the "happy pagan."

Quoting Hebrews 11:6 as justification for the subjective point, Pinnock writes, "According to Hebrews, it is faith or subjective religion which God is concerned about" (ibid.). But this verse leaves out all adherents to theistic views who do not subscribe to a biblical, personal theism of God's existence ("must believe that he is") and who do not believe that He responds ("is a rewarder of those who seek him"). We have no problem with God's concern for people in alternate worldviews. We do have problems with His being concerned only about their "faith or subjective religion." Why? Their non-Christian, religious worldview interpretively filters their "faith or subjective religion" in their search for the biblical God. A

Christian doctrine of conversion solidly contests the inclusivist proposal. If people turned to God from idols (1 Thess. 1:9), what kind of turning was it? Could they keep the subjective part of their supposed faith relationship to the true God while exchanging the objective component of their commitments with the biblical God? Conversion does not relate merely to interchangeable objective components of belief. It includes the appropriate subjective response to the Christian object of belief.

Also observe some details of Romans 10:1–3 on this subject. Paul's blood brethren, the people of Israel, had zeal for God (subjective religion) but not in accordance with knowledge (objective religion). Verse 3 clearly portrays the danger of "not knowing about God's righteousness." Such a "subjective religion" leads to unbelievers seeking to establish their own righteousness and not subjecting themselves to the righteousness of God. Jewish piety and zeal did not keep Paul from wishing for their salvation (v. 1). So, subjective religion does not seem to be the Bible's main concern. A total-person religion within the framework of appropriate knowledge is the Bible's main concern. Even a short examination of John 4, Romans 10:1–3, and Hebrews 11:6 renders the following statement erroneous, "What God really cares about is faith and not theology, trust and not orthodoxy" (*WGM*, 112. Earlier Pinnock wrote, "The fact that different kinds of believers are accepted by God proves that the issue for God is not the content of theology but the reality of faith" [105]. Later he reiterates, "the issue God cares about is the direction of the heart, not the content of theology" [158; cited earlier].). This kind of statement is only feasible if too strong a division is made between objective and subjective religion. The position that a person may be subjectively right with God but objectively wrong is not biblically or theologically defensible. God cares about faith and theology, trust and orthodoxy.

As one can discern, the inclusivist position inclines to a "least common denominator" view of theological truth and the highest common denominator view of existential faith. Instead, I propose a highest common denominator of existential *need*. Existential need is one of several constitutional needs that exist because of humanness. These needs are filled by the only common denominator of a theological solution, the Lord Jesus Christ. Pinnock is right when he says, "There are so many evil sides to religion that a fulfillment paradigm (the idea that religions point people to Christ) is out of the question" (*WGM*, 91). But what he seems to convey, is an "infillment" paradigm —the idea that people can find the true God within their life orbit (religions included), outside of Jesus Christ, as God fills their life. I propose the "answer" paradigm of religions. Jesus Christ is the solution to all the spiritual, intellectual, emotional, existential questions that humanness, in all its dimensions, causes people to ask. These are the same questions all humans ask at different levels and in different ways regardless of which culture and religion they belong to. They are the questions that non-Christian religions seek to answer but, to differing degrees, fail to do so. They completely fail to answer people's ultimate redemptive search.

I conclude this section by adding that I am not naively positive about the religiosity of Christians and negative about the religiosity of everybody else (*WGM*, 83; cited earlier). Even those who supposedly possess "full-strength salvation" are highly disappointing in their behavior and attitudes. I am just positive about the means and ground of the salvation Christ offers, and negative about non-Christian means and grounds of salvation.

False and True Religion

Pinnock first considers the dark side of religion to assure evangelicals that he sees that dark side too (*WGM*, 87). For instance, he pursues a "morality" evaluation of non-Israelite and Israelite religion in the Old Testament (*WGM*, 87–89). He notes that Jesus, Paul, and the New Testament also criticize religion. As noted above, Pinnock discounts a "fulfillment" paradigm of religions: "Part of a responsible theology of religions must be an unambiguous judgment against idols of our creation and deceptions of the Evil One" (*WGM*, 91).

Salvific Truth and Human Behavior. However, Pinnock's section on false religion obscures the distinction between false religion and false practitioners of true beliefs. A critique of Israel's religion falls under the latter category. The prophets and Jesus could not criticize Israel's blindness unless there was a true religion to which the nation did not attain. It is no wonder that Pinnock contends that, "one can go to hell as easily from church as from temple or mosque" (*WGM*, 90). But wrong observance of religions does not tell us anything about the salvific nature or value of those religions. All it tells us (and non-Christian religious leaders tell us too) is that good religion may be corruptly followed. A morality evaluation of religions is a case of an invalid ad hominem (against the person) argument. The religiosity of adherents is not a means to evaluate the verity of the religion. Irish Catholics and Protestants, Muslim Shiites and Sunnis, Hindu Brahmins and Harijans, have a way to escape the charge of theological error if their morality is the chief criterion for evaluating their truth claims. Actually, a Jew or Muslim could have written Pinnock's section on false religion. It is bereft of implications for salvific truth.

Pinnock affirms that true (non-Yahwist/non-Christian) religion, on the other hand, is recognized by the Bible under the terms of the wider covenant made with Noah. "It recognizes faith, neither Jewish nor Christian, which is nonetheless noble, uplifting, and sound" (*WGM*, 92). He repeats the "pagan saint" argument in support of this assertion. We have already critiqued his examples, use, and interpretation of the "pagan saint" theme in chapter 2. But he introduces the fact of Israelite borrowing from Near Eastern religions (*WGM*, 93–94) as another piece of evidence that there are positive features in non-Israelite religion.

Salvific Truth and Israelite Borrowing. Our interaction with the use of the "borrowing" position hovers around two related questions. What did Israel borrow? What does such borrowing prove? First, the phenomenon of borrowing occurs in several places in Scripture. For instance, there are formal similarities (such as the literary genre of prophecy) between the book of Revelation and late Jewish apocalyptic literature.[10] As such, Scripture is not an anti-cultural isolate. Biblical writers lived in contact with and were influenced by their surroundings.[11] Second, there were major "positive features" regarding non-salvific matters in those surrounding cultures and religions. Scripture authors had no problem with that kind of borrowing. The problem comes when such borrowing is alledged to infer salvific content in those cultures and religions. Third, if the corporate, vocational, elective purpose of promoting YHWH among the nations was to be accomplished by the Israelites, they had to interact with their neighbors. "Borrowing" enabled them personally to adapt and communicate concretely their hope in Yahweh to surrounding communities. Fourth, some events, such as the Creation and the Flood, were international in scope and effect. One would expect accounts of it in non-revelatory sources around the world.[12] Also, the "borrowing" need not always be one-sided. Historical existence causes a dynamic exchange of ideas, truths, and falsities between nearby cultures.[13] Fifth, it is possible to be taken up with the borrowing feature without being critical about what was left out or modified or sanctioned. Non-Jewish/Christian views of *redemption* were simply not adopted and sanctified. "Beliefs or practices rejected by Israel were always rejected on some solid theological ground."[14]

It would be blind and naive not to recognize positive features in non-Christian religions. Pinnock asks, "Is there evidence in the Bible for seeing *any* positive features in the religious aspects of cultures due to God working in this sphere?" (*WGM*, 93). Those of us who were reared and live in non-Christian majority environments (which environment is not?) appreciated and absorbed the behavioral insight, practical wisdom, moral ambition, cumulative knowledge, cultural assumptions, philosophical shrewdness, and social prudence of our surroundings. All we protest is the assertion that God is salvifically working *within* them to provide redemption *outside* explicit knowledge of Jesus Christ. Instead, we relate God's salvific working in non-Christian religions to the Spirit's pre-evangelistic activity of convicting the world of sin, righteousness, and judgment in preparation for the gospel. The question to inclusivists is still unyielding: Are non-Christian religions saving, in the Christian sense? To say that the Bible "recognizes faith . . . noble, uplifting and sound" (*WGM*, 92) in non-Christian religions is to go beyond biblical parameters. There are noble, uplifting, and sound elements in the religions. They even enhance the Christian's appreciation of the scriptural worldview.[15] However, to posit "noble, uplifting and sound *faith*" toward Christian salvation as available in these religions is inadmissible.

Inclusivists have already broadened the content of saving faith, the saving role of God outside and beyond the Incarnation, and the constituents of the saved to a variety of believers. Now, they have to broaden the character of salvation to include positive features in other religions. The obstacle to the broadening is that although religions are salvific in intent, phenomena, and claims, they do not cater to a common, generic salvation. Braaten makes a germane point,

> The proper business of religion is to save, but not all salvation is the same. . . . No generic salvation exists, no salvation to which the various religions can merely provide different labels. . . . The history of religions provides us with different models of salvation and different ways that the models are supposed to work. Each religion advertises the particular salvation it promises those who are willing to follow its way.[16]

A distinctive biblical orbit of salvation would include non-temporal election, divine love and grace, Christ's cross and its immediate and eternal effects, the role of the Spirit, the hearing of the gospel, the response of faith, and so on.[17] It is this salvific orbit that is completely unique to the Christian faith. A religion is *salvifically* true as it corresponds to biblical salvation. This biblical salvation is not found in non-Christian religions. Therefore, these religions cannot provide an extraordinary way or vehicle of salvation for their adherents.[18]

Inclusivists also broaden the existence of the concept of the high Creator God to various religions that may have similar concepts.

> The proof that people commonly intend the same deity as Christians worship is seen when the Bible is translated into languages of the world. The word "God" normally can be rendered by a word already known to the people in their own languages as referring to the same Supreme Being. People fear God all over the world, and God accepts them, even where the gospel of Jesus Christ has not yet been proclaimed. (*WGM*, 97)

I first address this issue from a translators' viewpoint and then will make a couple of more philosophical comments. Historically, most Bible translators seem to have been very conscious about choosing God-words that were not inimical to the biblical doctrine. For example, Brahman, the dominant word for the absolute, is not found in any Indian translation of the Christian Scriptures (neither do Shiva, Vishnu, etc., occur). Deva, which may show relationship to the Greek *theos,* was much more conducive to the Christian concept and is used extensively. Is this any different a technique from that of the biblical writers who borrowed words, often emptied them of non-Christian concepts, and filled them with distinctive Christian content for theologizing and contextualizing (cf. *theos, agape,* and numerous other Greek words)?

So, translators use local terminology for communicating and clarifying Christian concepts (e.g., heaven, hell, salvation, evil, etc.), and sometimes they create words simply by transliterating them (e.g., English "baptism"). When translators merely find an extant word for God (or any other Christian concept) in a local language, it does not mean that those who used the word believed in the same or true God.[19]

But philosophically, inclusivist anxiety to see similarities and ties between Christianity and the religions forces them into a "parallelism" mode of thinking. Many writers on comparative religion fall into this trap of finding trans-cultural and trans-religious parallels between and among religions. By doing this they tend to overlook divergences and contradictions between the parallels. For instance, inclusivists see the same God, ultimately, in each of the comparative religions. Let me suggest a few logical difficulties with this view.

First, Pinnock and other writers on comparative religion are guilty of hasty generalization. This is the rule that Pinnock uses to show that similar high, creator God concepts in Judaism, Islam, and Ghanaian religion prove an identity and identification of the true God in these religions. Pinnock notes,

> When Jews and Muslims, for example, praise God as the Creator of the world, it is obvious that they are referring to the same Being. We may assume that they are intending to worship the one Creator God that we also serve. . . . If people in Ghana speak of a transcendent God . . . how can anyone conclude otherwise than that they intend to acknowledge the true God as we do? (*WGM*, 97)

This statement is not only too small a sample of religions, theologies, and words, it also makes too superficial a comparison. It overlooks divergences and actual collisions in core doctrines between religions. Those who generalize in comparative religion assume that similarity of teaching and frequency of occurrence points to or proves identical thought or even common origin. Perhaps we may learn something of non-Christian views on such generalization from a recent non-Cristian enactment. "Malaysian Government authorities in Johor Bahru banned the use of Islamic words in non-Islamic religions. The word for God in the local language is 'Allah.' Evangelicals say Christian publishing, including

Bibles, stands imperiled."[20] Apparently, Malaysian Muslims recognize distinctions that inclusivists (and some Bible translators!), by saying that at least two great monotheistic religions worship the same God, do not. Courtesy and theology demands that we give credence to non-Christians' differentiation between themselves and the Christian faith. Perhaps this kind of courtesy was evident in the observations about the second World Parliament of Religions with which we opened this chapter.

Second, wherever there is the comparative attempt at "broadening" the content of core doctrines to show parallelism, all kinds of reductionism are present and are needed to promote the position. My previous point concerning the overlooking of creedal divergences manifests an "effect reductionism" of sorts. This is the process by which one reduces the "effects" in his anxiety to posit a common cause and common factor between the religions. An evolutionary view of origins seems to be assumed and applied to the sphere of religions—as the singular model of explaining origins. Even if the name or word for God is borrowable or identical, a "common source fallacy" is apparent. For example, we have borrowable, translatable, and highly interchangeable words for father across cultures, religions, languages, and worldviews. This does not mean all people are referring to the same person even though children across cultures exhibit a similar affection for the person who is called "father." Further, there is some cross-cultural correspondence in parental functions and roles. However, it is not possible to take these functional and emotional correspondences and interchange them. The parental functions and emotions of the offspring may be similar, but these have little to say about equating the persons in reference.

We may see the fallacy of this "common cause" point from a more interesting angle. My wife's father is "Jack," whom she calls "Dad." A close friend's father is "Jack," whom he also calls "Dad." If one forces the inclusivist point about borrowable and translatable "God-concepts," both Jacks would refer to the same person! However, a definition of the *person* of the two dads (for example, their last names) indicates two different persons in description and reality.

A popular illustration of the other logical fallacy mentioned above—the "common factor fallacy"—also comes to mind. After a football win, one university fraternity got drunk with beer and water;

another with brandy and water; another with gin and water; and a fourth with whiskey and water. Obviously, the common factor for the sophomoric drunkenness was the water from the university's water system!

Pinnock's suggestions about the word for God are statements that are not exact or definitive in content. He has jumped from an observation of the phenomenon of religions to making normative theological judgments. These judgments arise without the profit of theological or functional critiques from the Christian or non-Christian sides.

Also, a standard reductive fallacy is evident. Inclusivists minimize the unique, holistic, theoretical, and practical relationships among worldview, religion, and culture in a non-Western religion.[21] This worldview-religion-culture correlation makes each religion a unique conceptualization of reality, a philosophical whole, and a complex entity. A religion is minimized when an essential strand of doctrine is picked out in order to make superficial comparisons with a doctrine in another religion. Inclusivists attempt to explain a major complexity in terms of just one of the many facets of a religion, namely, "the Supreme Being Concept." But, the animistic high-god seems closer to the Muslim Satan than to the biblical God. And the Muslim God portrays a "monism of divine will" when compared to personalistic theism. The existence of a supreme being in different religions is far from proving that people "intend the same deity." In this kind of comparative religion, "God" becomes a victim of language as mere symbolization.

I hasten to note that an adaptation of the theistic, ontological argument is hidden here. From God-concepts in these religions, inclusivists argue for the *existence* of the same God in truth and belief. As such, the criticisms of the ontological argument for the existence of God is applicable to this adaptation too. To strengthen his argument, the inclusivist could use this adaptation of the ontological argument to establish the nature of God. The reader will notice later that the adaptation of ontological argument strengthens the evangelical case in establishing a stronger inference from general revelation for the God who is high, perfect, powerful, and wise.

Another reductionism relates to lessening the function of the doctrine of God in these other religions. Indeed, even if the concept of the supreme being is present, it does not play the same role in the religions. Pinnock falls into a variation of the unfairness criticism that he levied against pluralists, "It [relativism] rules out people's most precious beliefs in things normative" (*WGM*, 70). Pinnock does not seem to be aware that he is not serious enough about beliefs that adherents of the religions are serious about. He forgets the ingressive quality and content of these God-teachings in the various religions. The Buddhistic core beliefs concerning the aggregate role of God and that role's place in a Buddhist worldview is very different from the Christian view of God's aggregate role. Pinnock recognizes this difference and yet wants to be optimistic. For instance, note: "In other words, I think we should not overemphasize the impersonal character of Buddha's faith. Of course, Buddhism is not Christianity and it does not try to be. But how does one come away after encountering Buddhism and deny that it is in touch with God in its way?" (*WGM*, 100).

Third, there is an implicit begging of the question by inclusivists in their understanding of the relationship of the supreme being to the religions. The existence of the same supreme being in various religions, languages, and cultures is proved by words they have for it. Consequently, the supreme being authenticates its existence *and* the words for it (see earlier citation in text, from *WGM*, 97). With this reasoning, we end up with the existence of the supreme being proving the existence of the words and the existence of the words proving its existence.[22] Inclusivists need to prove that the supreme being should be the necessary or sufficient cause of this linguistic phenomenon. The 1993 World Parliament of Religions illustrates our point. Hans Kung, an eminent authority on Christianity and world religions, acknowledged the difficulty in interreligious agreements as he worked for a year on preparing the statement for the Parliament, "I never worked so many months for so few words."[23] The document was to extract a *common* ethic from existing religious traditions but could not use the word God as part of that commonality. To suggest that the concept of God is the same in divergent religions simply because they have linguistically translateable words for God is to trivialize, superficialize, and generalize God. Serious attempts at interreligious communication and clarification point to another conclusion than inclusivists envision.

Fourth, there is so much ambiguity and equivocation (language fallacies such as unintentional ambiguity and/or intentional equivocation)[24] in this connection between God and the religions that it reflects badly on the logic of inclusivism. We are first asked to consider "positive features" of the religions (*WGM*, 93ff.). But inclusivists make a jump from "positive" features to equate them with "salvific" features. God's work in the wider world is equated with God's salvific work. Truth and goodness are equated with *saving* truth and goodness.

Is there an alternate explanation of these parallels in religions that is biblically and logically consistent and evangelically authentic? The following discussion should have some implications for the origin and truth content of religions.

Existentially, if religions hope to answer similar existential, physiological, and philosophical questions, then similar answers may be expected. Mankind is a religious bunch with a religious hunch—an innately religious population that creates meaning-filled and meaningful words for the supreme being.

Anthropologically, the human make-up needs a God-crutch, a God-filling, and a God-standard for its existence, purpose, and morality. For this reason an occasional parity of the religions with the Christian faith may be explained. A deficient human-constitution (including the defaced image of the true God and the implant of a human conscience in every human being) gropes after God and salvation. Each human is at a different stage of spiritual response to general revelation and the pre-evangelistic conviction of the Holy Spirit in his life.

Theologically, people's actual and theoretical interaction with general revelation provides enough cause for similarity among the answers (Rom. 1). Here is a genesis for world religions. Moral, sensitive, and wise people (and communities) at different levels of appropriate or inappropriate response to general revelation have created or become the fountainheads of religions. This is how we explain that some religions are *ethically* closer to Christianity than others are. However, special, normative, divine revelation is needed for salvific truth. Conceptual or ethical approximations of the Christian God-concept are not enough to save.

So, Christians and non-Christians do not gain much by broadening their core concepts to make parallels between religions. Inclusivists and pluralists have to, by necessity, see structural parallels for an innate connection between world religions. We promote an external parallelism for the purposes of illustration and analogy in communicating the gospel. (From personal interaction, I surmise that Don Richardson in *Eternity in Their Hearts* was surfacing this kind of external parallelism as natural analogies and points of contact for communicating Christ cross-religiously and cross-culturally. Even though he has opened himself up for criticism, he does not seem to hold that these analogies, in their own right, are containers of redemptive truth, sufficient for any aspect of Christian salvation.)

General Revelation, Special Revelation, and World Religions. The relationship between general and special revelation needs to be addressed. General revelation as the mediator of salvation is a strong tenet of the inclusivist, wider hope position. In contrast to the traditional "negative" view "that God gives it [general revelation] to ensure the damnation of sinners and not their salvation" (*WGM*, 104), "any one can find God at anywhere any time, because he has made himself and his revelation accessible to them."[25] We may agree with the general force of the immediate citation, but how people find God and salvation in general revelation remains the question. What is the exact role of general revelation and its relationship to special revelation?

First, general revelation plays a negative role. God's invisible attributes, eternal power, and divine nature have been clearly seen since the creation of the world "so that mankind is without excuse" (Rom. 1:20). General revelation is not so much to ensure damnation, but to justify damnation to those who could have responded to it but would excuse themselves on the basis of ignorance.

Second, general revelation plays a positive role in accounting for the origin, maintenance, and development of religions. The interaction between general revelation and the human tendency to seek transcendence produces comprehensive and sophisticated religio-cultural means for mankind to exist and prosper.

So, although general revelation plays a positive role in sustaining mankind, it does not play a mediatorial role in saving mankind. Think through a control belief of the inclusivist that "God uses general revelation to mediate his salvific grace" (*NON*, 233). Inclusivists may excel at criticizing pluralism, but they fall prey to their own criticism. The pluralist dogma of modernity teaches that "it would be unfair for truth not to be equally and simultaneously present to everyone. . . . [We] have to assume that ultimate reality is known vaguely by everyone, even if not clearly by anyone" (*WGM*, 70). Is it not because of this pluralist dogma that inclusivists propose their modified theory in the first place? "General revelation mediating God's grace" is clearly based on the second assumption in the above quote. "Mediatorial" general revelation supposedly presents truth equally and simultaneously to everyone. There is one God and one mediator between God and men, namely, general revelation. General revelation has assumed the role of Christ.

Third, the relationship between general and special revelation is one of both quantity and difference. Inclusivists see all revelation on a continuum of salvation, with salvation being found anywhere on the continuum.[26] Responding in faith to general revelation and the pre-evangelistic work of the Spirit makes one a *pre-Messianic* believer. Responding in faith to special revelation makes one a *Messianic* believer with full-strength salvation (*WGM*, 105).

Now, the Bible permits the heavens to declare the attributes of God indisputably through His creative activity (Ps. 19:1; Rom. 1:19–20) and man's understanding of them. "That which is known about God is evident within them; for *God* made it evident to them. . . . They knew God" (Rom. 1:19, 21, italics added). However, general revelation does not declare the salvific attributes and activities of God. That is, nature may show us the provision, wisdom, and power of God, but not the love of God. The lamb may be sucking on the ewe's breast, even as a lion tears into it. It takes special revelation to declare to us the love of God. General revelation can lead men to special revelation. It will lead all those who throw themselves on God and His basic truths to Jesus Christ's wishes and initiative on their behalf. But general revelation cannot save. It will justify one's eventual condemnation.

Also, the distinction inclusivists make between pre-Messianic believers and Messianic believers is itself quite dubious. (Sanders too makes a comparable distinction between believers and Christians [*NON*, 224ff.].) It is hard biblically to maintain the distinction. For instance, one of their favorite verses reads, "God the Savior of all men, especially of believers" (1 Tim. 4:10). The extent of the distinction in this verse is between all people and believers. The verse would have to be rewritten as follows to accommodate the inclusivist distinction: "God the Savior of all believers and especially of Christians." But then the first part would sound restrictivist. Or, they would have to qualify the verse further as "God the Savior of all men, especially of believers, and particularly of Christians." Either way there is major difficulty in distinguishing between believers (pre-Messianic believers) and Christians (Messianic believers)—a pillar distinction necessary to maintain the inclusivist thesis.

Pinnock's use of Acts 14:16–17 in connection with the issue of mediatorial general revelation is informative and selective (*WGM*, 104). He is anxious to emphasize the second part of the verse, "God has not left himself without testimony," but not the first part, "in the past, God let all nations go their own way." This "past" is the past time that provides inclusivist support for persons' coming to God by general revelation and prevenient grace. However, the text says all nations (including Israel) have been going their own way rather than coming to God through the Noahic covenant or the Abrahamic covenant. And God let them go their own way, instead of moving in with the universal, salvific will for the masses. Apparently, part of "God's dialogue with the nations" was to let them go their own way. Also, Pinnock interprets "testimony" in this passage to mean, "Elements of truth and goodness exist in pagan cultures like theirs because God has been with them and has not failed to reveal himself to them" (*WGM*, 96). But the "testimony" here is clearly one of sustenance and common grace: providential supply of rain and food, which results in their fullness of life. How Pinnock gets this text to mean "truth and goodness in pagan cultures" is extremely difficult to see.

Earlier he asks, "Why are we so reluctant to accept that God is in dialogue with other nations?" (*WGM*, 29). Traditional evangelicals are not reluctant at all, if Pinnock admits all of the biblical text into that divine-international dialogue. But such an admission is not fully promising for salvific purposes only. Letting nations go their own way does not seem to be a "gracious and understanding appreciation of their past and their culture" (cf. Pinnock's earlier comment on these verses [*WGM*, 32]). Combine these two verses with the recurrent theme of "God giving mankind over" (Rom. 1:24, 26, 28) and it is difficult to corroborate the conclusion only with "God is committed to full racial salvation" (*WGM*, 19. By the way, Pinnock does not use Romans 1–2 in his treatment of Paul's critique of religion [*WGM*, 89–90].). "Letting nations go their own way" (Acts 14:16–17) is consistent with "God giving them up" (Rom. 1).

Here, a comment on the inclusivist distinction between kinds of believers as related to their respective accessibility to different kinds of salvific revelation is appropriate. The distinction yields an improbable division between kinds of biblical salvation. Pre-Messianic believers are said to relate to mediatorial general revelation and receive (eventual) salvation. Messianic believers, on the other hand, relate to revelation about Jesus, and receive full-strength salvation for this earthly life. "Unevangelized believers need a clearer revelation of God's love and forgiveness and the assurance that goes with love and forgiveness" (*WGM*, 179). "Jesus alone can give them: the Holy Spirit, a portion in the kingdom of God, and the experience of messianic salvation" (ibid.).

However, Acts 14:17 portrays an opposite connotation of the benefits of the time and quality of salvation. A theistic God (cf. present pre-Messianic believers) fills hearts with *this-worldly* food and gladness. The consistent testimony of Scripture is that believing in Jesus results in more than a this-worldly strength for this life only. For example, in 1 Corinthians 15:19 (NIV) Paul writes, "If only for this life we have hope in Christ, we are to be pitied more than all men." Inclusivists would like Jesus' full-strength salvation to make a real difference only in earthly life. If that is so, Christians (and Christianity), according to the apostle, are to be most pitied among all men.

Fourth, special revelation is specific and contains more information than general revelation. General revelation tells about God's handiwork, but it does not tell about man's sinfulness, God's love, the cross, and the reception of its benefits. As such, special revelation adds different kinds of information to the seeker of God's salvation. Special revelation communicates full-strength salvation, but general revelation does not offer half-strength salvation. General revelation enables mankind to cope; special revelation enables mankind to hope. General revelation helps mankind survive; special revelation helps mankind thrive now and forever.

Unfortunately, the grading of revelation according to the specifics of information yields to inclusivist assumptions that mankind's problem is based on an intellectual departure from God—a departure substantially solved by adequate information that general revelation communicates. However, mankind's problem is comprehensive and debilitating, including moral and volitional aspects of spiritual departure. The fool has said in his heart, not just in his head, that there is no God (Ps. 14:1). We hold that though special revelation is a crucial element of the salvific process, it does not save by itself. There are many who have the advantage of salvific details who simply are not saved. Inclusivists use the intellectual element of ignorance and inaccessibility to raise the entire issue against evangelicals, but then accuse evangelicals of intellectualising missions and salvation. (Contrary to Sanders's suggestion that evangelicals see missions as informational [he garners Charles Kraft's models to support the thesis, *NON*, 267], the wider-hope arguments against evangelicals and their proposals are built on the "information" issue. Again, evangelicals maintain intellectual, moral, and volitional components to the sin and salvation sequence.)

I conclude this section with the primary question: Do those who respond rightly to general revelation receive salvation from its content? In addition to the biblical and theological comments above, I make the well-known philosophical distinction between necessary and sufficient causation.[27] For those steeped in non-Christian traditions, general revelation is a necessary step toward receiving salvific reward—the one who wishes to come to God and believes that He exists (Heb. 11:6). But the sufficient cause of that person's faith in Christ is special revelation. That is, general revelation by its absence could prevent special revelation and faith in Christ for salvation; but could not, without special revelation, cause faith in Christ for salvation merely by its presence. General revelation promises God's reward of salvation. It takes special revelation actually to participate in salvation's reward.

I illustrate the concept in the context of world religions. Religions are candlelights by which people live. "Positive features" of the candlelights include their reality and usefulness in a morally dark universe. Some candles are brighter and longer lasting than others. But candlelight is not sunlight. Sunlight is different in amount and kind from candlelight. At the brightness of the sun, candles are not necessary for light. Further, candles are not lit nor do they stay lit by the sun. Just as candles have purposes other than light (e.g., heat and ornamentation), religions have other good purposes. But nobody lives or must live by candlelight when sunlight is unrestrained and effusive. World religions may be appreciated for practical benefits and aesthetic beauty. Sunlight helps us appreciate candles and candlemakers. But candle *light* is not needed along with sunlight for light. We appreciate religions and their positive features. We just do not accept the saving content of structure of non-Christian religions. Anyone lighting a candle by day is doing it for other than light.

"CHRIST AS VICTOR" THEME

In a chapter devoted to "Religions Tomorrow," Pinnock addresses a biblical philosophy of history and its impact on religious dialogue. "Truth-seeking dialogue" is legitimate because everything, including religions, is changing and "God has designs on them" (*WGM*, 116). So, Pinnock looks forward to God's historical transformation of world religions even as He brings in the kingdom and realizes worldwide sovereignty (ibid.). The "Christ as Victor" theme is asserted to prove that God may be at work changing religions as one of the powers over which Christ won His victory (*WGM*, 119–22). Thus there can be a good syncretism and truth-seeking dialogue between Christianity and the religions.

This view requires a meta-religious God standing above and beyond all religions, including Christianity, judging and transforming them. (See the section on the "Contest of the Gods," beginning on p. 122 of *WGM*.) The existence (and concept) of a meta-religious God outside the bounds of the Christian religion is antithetical to the evangelical faith. Evangelicals gladly posit an exclusive God who judges all people, including Christians, and who will establish His victory over all powers. Furthermore, they can agree that the accomplishments of the cross by Christ the Victor are broad and pervasive. The victory theme applies to all entities from civilizations to supernatural powers (*WGM*, 119). But Pinnock needs to relate the victory theme integrally to the common substitutionary theme of the cross in relationship to world religions. The problem is that the substitutionary theme is narrow and personal. Also, the view of a meta-religious God outside Christianity sees the Christian faith merely as a cultural and social phenomenon and not as the unique redemptive ground and exclusive redemptive means for all people from any religion. The critical issue is if God's redemptive means as revealed in Christ is also a changing dynamic in an inclusivist philosophy of history, if "everything in history is forever changing" (*WGM*, 115). Is salvation through Christ a static or changing precept?

Pinnock illustrates the triumph of God over the powers by changes in religion. For example, God has triumphed over the ancient Near Eastern deities as well as the quasi-religion of Marxism. These religions have failed gods. The fall of Marxism (the great quasi-religion) is evidence of God's winning the victory (*WGM*, 124–25; Pinnock may be equating what is secularly considered to be the sheer impact of market forces with God's victory over Communism, thus leaving one to conclude that a triumphant Western orientation is on God's victory side [cf. his "humanizing features that belong to the Western democracies owing to a degree of Christianization," *WGM*, 120]). This victory note is probably premature, however. Look at what has replaced ancient Near Eastern religion. The most anti-Christian (even worse than Marxism) of all attitudes in history dominates this geographical area. History has seen the Christianity of this locale nearly removed. Pinnock may also consider what has replaced the area once dominated by the vibrant churches of Revelation 2–3. If victory is determined by which god occupies a geographical area, the Christian God is not presently in triumph in the Middle East. Pinnock's prayer that "Christ will soon confront Islam and that she will open up to the Gospel for the sake of her peoples" (*WGM*, 126) may be echoed by all believers, but it is meaningless and powerless in terms of the "wider-hope." For according to this theory, Muslims too may be in heaven with just enough heart response to the true Creator God outside Christ. Why this new vision of the Christian faith has more "transforming power" (ibid.) is not clear. The same optimism toward historical transformation may be advanced from a traditional view without widening the way of salvation. Actually, why is a transformation of these religions necessary at all, if indeed non-Christians may find eternal salvation within those religious contexts? Also, if some of their non-Christian religion is accounted for by the operations of the divine Logos and the pre-incarnate Spirit, why should their religions undergo historical transformation as they relate to redemption?

TRUTH-SEEKING DIALOGUE

Truth-seeking dialogue is "important to Christ's impacting other religions" (*WGM*, 129–30). But this truth-seeking dialogue is not defined. What kind of truth are Christians to seek? Again we find that Pinnock pursues the biblical basis for truth-seeking encounters on a dubitable footing. He uses Jesus in the temple, at age twelve, as a model for truth-seeking encounter (Luke 2:41–52).

Jesus sits "among them, listening to them and asking them questions" (*WGM*, 130). Were Jesus' questions in search of truth? The text notes that He was astonishing the leaders with His understanding and answers. Also, Pinnock erroneously uses Pauline engagement in dialogue for the sake of evangelism to model a truth-seeking strategy of missions. There is no hint in the text that Paul was seeking for truth; Paul was *propounding* truth.

Pinnock holds that one may "test their [non-Christian religious] claims for any rational, moral, or religious power they may possess to make sense of things" (*WGM*, 116). This is where he begins in truth-seeking dialogue, but he ends up finding redemption in the religious claims. There is no problem looking for rational insight, moral enlightenment, and religious solutions to common human dilemmas in which Christians and non-Christians find themselves. However, to find rational, moral, and religious power *toward redemption* is pointless. (Earlier Pinnock takes the optimism of salvation to include optimism toward salvific truth in the religions: "How does one come away after encountering Buddhism and deny that it is in touch with God in its way?" [*WGM*, 100; italics added]). The uniqueness and exclusiveness of redemptive truth must be preserved in such dialogue. Christians may affect other religions in dialogue, but we do not make an impact on them by seeking for redemptive truth in them. Interreligious dialogue is not necessarily truth-seeking dialogue.[28] Truth-seeking dialogue, as perceived by the inclusivists, is based on the idea that all human beings share fundamental notions (universal common ground) and that once we dig out this core we shall attain the truth. Unfortunately in this process, "the integrity of the various particular traditions is violated in order to cram them into these preconceived patterns."[29]

Later, Pinnock writes, "Evangelicals cannot forsake the finality of Christ, but they can try harder to do justice to non-Christian truths and values" (*WGM*, 139). How would the evangelical know these are non-Christian "truths," except as they do not collide with or are neutral to Scripture? If so, then they are Christian truths too. And if I read Pinnock right, some non-Christian values that are not approved by Scripture are not worth pursuing, e.g., bribery, corruption, and so forth. However, Scripture is the standard. Perhaps he needs to reword his statement in this manner: Christians must try harder to do justice to non-salvific truths in non-Christian religions.

Syncretism (blending elements between Christianity and another religion) is another subject that must be brought up here. Almost always, evangelicals have spoken about syncretism in a negative way. Yet Pinnock speaks about a good syncretism in which, for instance, Christianity forces Buddhism to take this world more seriously. "On the other hand, Christians in the West need to become less materialistic and more spiritually Buddha-like" (*WGM*, 140). I presume that syncretism may function in a good way in non-salvific matters. But do Christians really need to go to Buddha, as Pinnock intimates, to become less materialistic? Also, do we really want to become more Buddha-like? We want to be more Christ-like. To the extent that Buddha looked like Christ, we may look like Buddha, but it is not because we want to become Buddha-like.

Pinnock's comments about the Buddha are syncretistically generous. "To mention examples of our own, how can one fail to appreciate the noble aspects of the Buddha, whose ethical direction, compassion, and concern for others is so moving that it appears God is at work in his life? Gautama resembles the sort of 'righteous man' whom Jesus told his disciples to receive (Mt. 10:41)" (*WGM*, 100). I agree that a Buddhistic reading of suffering and ethics is most profound, but is God *redeemingly* at work in Buddha's life? (Cf. his generous optimism toward Buddhism, cited earlier in the text from *WGM*, 100.) If Buddhism is "in touch with God in its way," is it in redemptive touch with the divine? If it is not, is this "in touch" of any eternal, redemptive consequence? Or can it be distinguished from the Christianity that Scripture holds is in touch with God in its own way? The answers Pinnock is suggesting have near heretical implications from an evangelical standpoint. Either Pinnock does not take Buddhism seriously (especially Buddhist exclusivity), or he does not want to accentuate dissimilarities, or he desires a least common denominator of faith to unite contradictory and divergent religions.

The particular passage he uses, Matthew 10:41, is one of the strongest passages on exclusivism for Jesus' disciples. Verses 32–33 specifically relate to whoever confesses and denies Christ. Verse 33 declares that Jesus has come to bring a sword. Jesus is the issue over all alternate possibilities for allegiance: families, siblings, parents (vv. 35–38). His disciples must follow after Him and lose their lives for His sake (v. 39). Jesus' disciples may receive prophets, righteous men, and children (vv. 41–42), but others must receive Him (v. 40). Now, do people receive Jesus when they receive Buddha (and receive Buddha when they receive Jesus), and do they thus receive the God who sent Jesus in this reception of Buddha (v. 40)?

Of necessity, a comprehensive philosophy of history will include the future.[30] In the context of the future of religions, Pinnock is presently at the position held by John Hick some decades ago. Hick "held out the possibility of something called eschatological verification, according to which we will all know the truth at least at the end of history. He was still sure that the personal and loving God of the Christian faith would be revealed as the true God in the end" (*WGM*, 135).[31] Pinnock, too, holds that the middle position between relativism and dogmatism in truth-seeking dialogue is epistemologically modest because "truth will be resolved eschatologically. This means that we will never fully resolve the conversation but patiently await the arrival of full knowledge from God."[32]

Other than the fact that this future scenario will be too late for most people in a Christian view of things, this is an agnostic position at best. Pinnock equates evangelicals' "finite, fragile ways" of truth as perhaps in error. He is not even willing to say that Christians shall be proved right eschatologically, only that a version of "religious pluralism will see an eschatological resolution" (*WGM*, 146). On an aside, we do understand the point that truth-seeking dialogue is epistemologically and ecclesiologically modest. Those who say they seek truth are usually more humble (at least on the outside) than those who display bumper stickers declaring, "I found it!" But such humility is nobler only if epistemological certainty must result in human pride. I agree there is a social modesty that follows uncertainty, but certainty itself does not need to demonstrate pride. Subsequently, there could also be a certainty about uncertainty in reversing the criticism. If religious roads are built by men, we had better be humble in accepting each other. However, if a religious road is built by God, it is inversely proud (pride disguised as humility) not to accept it.

THE ETERNAL DESTINY
OF THE UNEVANGELIZED

We now come to the thorny problem of "hope for the unevangelized." Inclusivists rightly rule out universalism. And for those who hold to conditional immortality the problematic issue of universalism does not arise. But pitting accessibility to the gospel against the urgency of missions is "a pressing problem for theology" (*WGM*, 150). Any access to the gospel eliminates the urgency of missions. The necessity of missions for salvation undermines the fairness issue. The issue is sensitive, horrific, and pathetic.

> The implication of popular eschatology is that the downtrodden of this world, unable to call upon Jesus through no fault of their own, are to be rejected for eternity, giving the final victory to the tyrants who trampled them down. Knowing little but suffering in this life, the unevangelized poor will know nothing but more and worse suffering in the next. (*WGM*, 152)

The inclusivist solution to the tough question includes a corporate election-redemption (but not universal salvation) rooted in God's boundless generosity, the pre-Christian faith-principle of the holy pagan paradigm, non-Christian actions of faith, the uncontested salvation-exception of infants and mentally incompetent, and the opportunity for a postmortem encounter with Christ.

I have dealt with several of these issues earlier in this work. For instance, the usefulness of the holy pagan paradigm for Pinnock's "manyness" thesis has already been questioned using other biblical passages. The pertinent texts indicate only a few (rather than many) coming to salvation through specific revelation (rather than through an abstract faith-principle). "The Bible says," Pinnock claims, "that there are true believers in the wider world who trust God and walk faithfully before him" (*WGM*, 22). At best, all that can be deduced from the pagan saint theme is that there *were* true believers in the wider world at times in the past. Most people in the pre-patriarchal and patriarchal time periods, to which inclusivists appeal for an ideology of salvific abundance, were judged rather than saved.

I have also dealt with the corporate aspects of election that inclusivists propose. From corporate election, they move on to a corporate emphasis for redemption and judgment. "Corporateness is visible when Jesus describes all nations (not individuals, one by one) gathering for judgment (Mt. 25:31–46)" (*WGM*, 151). They also see the eventual kingdom of Christ as sustaining the corporate emphasis, but how this relates to many coming to salvation is unexplained. Pinnock's conclusion is that "the Bible is more concerned about structural redemption than the fate of individuals in contrast to ourselves" (*WGM*, 152). We shall consider the Matthean text later, but most of the passages that inclusivists use speak about eschatological judgment rather than salvation. And promoting a corporate emphasis does not necessarily lead to an inclusivist position as some Barthian theologians would insist.[33] Let us now turn to other inclusivist material on the destiny of the unevangelized for interaction and critique.

God's Generosity and Accessibility

Inclusivists garner biblical support for God's generosity from such passages as the following. Johannine pictures of international salvation (Rev. 7:9; 11:13; 21:24, 26) "must include a substantial number of the unevangelized" (*WGM*, 153). Jesus spoke about an eschatological pilgrimage to a messianic banquet (Luke 13:29). "God is bringing many to glory, not a solitary few (Heb. 2:10)" (*WGM*, 154). When inclusivists speak of large numbers in an undefined or indefinite way, the biblical data may be used to prove either side of the position. For instance, a restrictivist may hold to the restrictivist condition of salvation rather than the restrictivist numbers of saved. Those who cannot meet the restrictivist condition (i.e., infants and mentally incompetent) of salvation may still be many, and therefore there can still be a large number fulfilling John's and Jesus' pictures of the end time.

Divine Resolve and Human Salvation. How does God's boundless generosity need to relate to the accessibility of salvation issue in the inclusivist proposal? "If God really loves the whole world and desires everyone to be saved, it follows logically that everyone must have access to salvation" (*WGM*, 157). But this is not a strong enough interpretation of God's real love and desire. It does not logically follow that everyone must only have access to salvation, but that everyone eventually must be saved. Pinnock already softens the intensity of "God's desire" from divine will to divine wish. (Restrictivist Augustinians have just softened "God's desire" a whole lot!) God's largeheartedness does not translate into universal salvation for inclusivists or Augustinians. The universalists score a major point here. Why should anyone be lost at all, for even if one is lost, then God's universal salvific will is stultified?

It is obvious there is tension in theology between what God would like to do and what He actually does when it comes to salvation. It is true that in every other realm of creation and providence, everything He would like to do, He can and will do. Does this compatibility between divine aspiration and action apply to salvation? The solemn matter is that both restrictivists and inclusivists operate from the same premise. Many restrictivists limit what God would like to do in salvation. Inclusivists enlarge what God can and will do to everything God would like to do in salvation.

Of course, this is a subset of the larger conversation between Calvinism and Arminianism and cannot be explored here.[34] The outlines of a probable solution acknowledge the tension as a factor arising from man's nature as "special" within God's creation. Man can override God's desire but not God's will. If he vetoes God's will, then God is less than sovereign and perfect. If God does not take into account man's freedom, then man is less than free. We combine these "limitations" of man and God with the nature of salvation as spiritual (i.e., salvation is in a "class" of its own—it occurs within nature but is not just natural; it is a supra-miracle on a metaphysical, supra-nature status) and arrive at the following conclusion. In the decisive issue of salvation, God's will is accomplished; but God's wishes are not (cf. Matthew 23:37: God wished to gather the children of Jerusalem but they were not willing). God's generosity is confined to a universal salvific *wish* and a universal salvific *welcome,* rather than expanded to a universal salvific *will.*

This seems to be the most consistent way to handle biblical material on the subject. It does not mean "God's universal salvific will implies the equally universal accessibility of salvation for all people" (*WGM*, 157). Pinnock quotes Stuart Hackett,

> If every human being . . . has been objectively provided for through the unique redemption in Jesus, and if this provision is in fact intended by God for every such human being, then it must be possible for every human individual to become personally eligible to receive that provision . . . since a universally intended redemptive provision is not genuinely universal unless it is also and for that reason universally accessible.[35]

Most evangelicals will have no major problem with Hackett's statement as it stands. The mechanics of salvation eligibility and accessibility are where the contention lies. The personal eligibility problem has been solved, for by Christ's redemption all men become savable from their condition of lostness.[36] Also, the phrase "universal accessibility" may be revised to "universal availability" of salvation to rid the statement of an "equal entitlement" connotation.

The issue of access has bearings on the fairness issue. An assumption in the inclusivist proposal is that God's desire to save everyone *obligates* Him to send the gospel message to everyone in the same way, to the same extent/amount, and with the same force. This is a rerun of a universalist premise on gospel access. Unless one is a universalist[37] (a position inclusivists rightly disavow), every other position is unfair and restrictivist to some extent. For example, is it not unfair that God gives Paul a dramatic heavenly vision but lets others respond to less-than-effective presentations of the gospel? Then there are others who do not hear the gospel at all. Who would not consider becoming a Christian if they were spectacularly and directly encountered by the heavenly Lord like Paul? Further, there are many kinds of rejecters. Passive rejecters (the inaccessible), the non-accepters (or neglecters of the great salvation), and the active rejecters (like Saul of Tarsus). Salvation and condemnation are multi-causal, and human observers simply do not have enough information to accuse the God of the evangelicals of unfairness. To some extent, any non-universalist scheme is unfair. However, once God's desire and decree (i.e., God's wish and God's will) in salvation are separated, the attraction of the modern view of equal rights and entitlements in relationship to this subject vanishes, or at least, substantially diminishes. While the generosity of God wishes and welcomes the salvation of all, the justice of God guarantees that no one will be saved or condemned unfairly. We are neither more generous nor more just than God. The generosity and justice of God protect everyone who should be in heaven from being in hell and disallow anyone in heaven who should not be there.

At this point, we must briefly look at inclusivist treatment of several related texts. First, there is the narrow road of Matthew 7:14. Pinnock understands this text to refer to a fewness doctrine of salvation, but he does not think "that this text about fewness can be used to cancel out the optimism of salvation that so many others articulate" (*NON*, 115–16). The problem with this adjustment of Matthew 7:14 is that it does not give the words and the verse's context enough force. The "two road" motif is entirely consistent with the two kinds of "professions" (7:21–23) and "builders" (7:24–29) of the rest of the chapter. God's generosity is tempered by verses 21–23, which make even the widest of narrow roads narrower—not even everyone who names the name of Christ will enter the kingdom of heaven.[38]

Second, Pinnock's treatment of the parable of the last judgment (Matt. 25) is also weak (*WGM*, 163–65). He examines the phrase "least of these brothers of mine" and discounts the "Christian missionaries" view and proposes "poor people as a whole" as qualifiers for the phrase. Following Jeremias, he proposes the "the hidden and unrecognized Messiah whom they encountered in the guise of the poor and suffering" (*WGM*, 164)—a view that can be referred to as the "anonymous Christ" view. He ignores or is unaware of a third option from the immediate eschatological context and the argument of Matthew—that Jewish Christians during the future period of global trouble are possibly in view. How the nations treat Jewish Christians at that time will be how they are treated at the judgment. He may need to consider the Matthean use of the brothers of Jesus to help determine the meaning of the phrase (cf. Matt. 12:50: "For whoever does the will of my Father who is in heaven, he is my brother"). In any case, he pursues a more personal than corporate judgment interpretation here, unlike the corporate emphasis he saw in this passage earlier (*WGM*, 151).

Third, Sanders' exegetical adjustments also pique my interest. Speaking about God's love for His children from Luke 15, he writes: "Our unusual God loves his children, including those whom we may consider particularly ungodly" (*NON*, 135). On two counts the parable does not lend support to the above conclusion. The straying son was already a son. He did not have to become a son. Sanders seems to say that God has children beyond His family. But, theological precision demands that people have to be brought into a child-father relationship with God, i.e., into God's family. Also, even if we grant Sanders' universalistically inclined interpretation, the straying child, to be welcomed home, still had to come to terms with the father's unchanging love and exclusive standards.

Human Incapacity and Divine Salvation. We now come to the issue of those unable to believe on the Lord Jesus Christ for their salvation. As one would expect, the salvation of those who die in infancy and that of the mentally incompetent is claimed for the wideness of salvation. "Since most Christians today grant that these people will be saved, they constitute a prime example of the unevangelized being saved apart from faith in Christ, apart even from faith in God in most cases" (*WGM*, 166). Sanders notes that "current attitudes toward children in Western civilization make the prospect of infant damnation unbearable" and that this sentimental reason may provide "considerable warrant" for the position (*NON*, 303). The weight of this observation is equal to his castigation of J. I. Packer's attributing "the American value of fairness" as influencing the universally accessible salvation position (ibid., 136).

First, Pinnock recognizes this exception to even his own condition of the faith-principle for salvation. All his pre-patriarchal and patriarchal holy pagans cannot support this exception. And if some may be excepted from this wider condition of faith in God, why could not others in the unevangelized areas of the world be excepted? The exceptive situation is not just a burden for traditional evangelicals. It is a burden for any salvation condition that is placed on humans, including the inclusivist's condition of seeking God. Second, I make a distinction between those who could not meet the salvation condition from those who can but will not meet the condition. Children who die[39] and the mentally incompetent fall into the former category and are not condemned.[40] When Pinnock asks, "Why so great a compassion for infants who cannot believe, and so little for large numbers of others perishing without God lifting a finger to save them?" (*WGM*, 167), he has answered the question. Infants who die and the mentally incompetent *cannot* respond to divine communication and believe; others do not believe because they *will not* respond to divine communication. Third, this excepted category of the saved has not established the excepted persons' personal guilt. These exceptions do show that people can be saved apart from faith in Christ. But it is because they could not have done so even if they had been presented the gospel.[41]

The theory of a special human messenger bringing the gospel to those who are rightly responding to the light they already have does not really solve "the size of the problem" (*WGM*, 166). Very few are known to have come to Christ in this way. In fact, most were not saved in this special messenger way in the Bible. We have dealt with the Cornelius issue earlier and cannot see it as lending weight to the inclusivist theory, let alone bringing large numbers into salvation. However, Cornelius does fit all the details of the special human messenger scenario, and as such gives us hope toward those who are sincerely seeking God. The promise of the reward of God's person (Heb. 11:6; cf. 2 Chron. 15:2, 24) applies to this position. God will get the gospel of Christ to the seeker in any possible way. Human messengers are the natural means of doing so. Divine messengers may be a supernatural means of doing so (Rev. 14:6). But, like Cornelius, all seekers must believe the gospel to receive salvation (Acts 10:43; 11:18). Certainly, if the motivation for soteriology and missiology is the "manyness" doctrine, then the special human messengers theory does not qualify. But the theory may not apply because large numbers are not seeking God even though they should be (Acts 17:27; Rom. 3:11b). In any case, the salvation of large numbers is not proved by isolated examples of individual pagans who were saved before Christ.

Christian Missions and the Issue of Urgency

How Wide Is God's Mercy? Inclusivist support for universal access to salvation also arises from the angle of a "grace-filled postmortem encounter." "Although the scriptural evidence for postmortem encounter is not abundant, its scantiness is relativized by the strength of the theological argument for it" (*WGM*, 169. Again, "The exegetical evidence may not be plentiful, but the theological argument is strong" [172].). As expected, Pinnock uses 1 Peter 3:19–20 for his primary, and only, scriptural plausibility.[42] He writes, "Scripture does not require us to hold that the window of opportunity is slammed shut at death" (*WGM*, 171). Postmortem encounters are meant for "babies dying in infancy" ("In the case of babies dying in infancy, the decision for God can come after death, since it could not have come before. This in turn may suggest that they are given time to grow up and mature, so then a decision could be made" [*WGM*, 168].), "those who sought God during their earthly lives and loved him" (*WGM*, 171), and pre-Messianic believers like Job who "will seal his faith by responding to Jesus" (*WGM*, 172).

Hebrews 9:27 is alluded to, but Pinnock does not deal with the force of its words. The death boundary is fixed in that verse. Of course, Hebrews 9:28 is even more definitive as to who will receive salvation: "those who are waiting for Christ to appear a second time." The force of both verses together shows there is no postmortem escape. In the Cornelius passage of Acts 10, the threat of divine judgment is part of the preaching to the people: "Jesus is the appointed judge of the living and the dead (cf. Acts 17:31, the other "religions" passage). Romans 2:5 reads, "you are storing up wrath against yourself for the day of God's wrath, when his righteous judgment will be revealed. God will give to each person according to what he has done" (cf. Rom. 2:16). These "judge and judgment" passages contain the negative motif of punitive retribution for the non-Christian rather than an opportunity for mercy in the judgment scenario.[43]

The fact is that "pre-Messianic believers" were already saved and were confident of being vindicated by their Redeemer (cf. Job 19:25). Old Testament believers were not under threat of eternal judgment. Indeed, their postmortem encounter with Jesus Christ will not be to confer salvation; otherwise the entire inclusivist argument for their pre-Christian salvation becomes meaningless. But there is another twist to my contention: If a person is really saved by the faith-principle, why a second, postmortem opportunity for salvation at all? Such a person would already be in heaven, experiencing the fullest strength of salvation. In spite of this postmortem delight in meeting Jesus, pre-Messianic believers do not need to receive the gospel for full-strength salvation.[44] Pre-Messianic believers do not need an opportunity to repent after death if they have already received salvation before death. (In spite of Pinnock's distrust of the divine "middle knowledge" argument, his description of postmortem opportunity has a curious "middle knowledge" sound to it: "The question is whether sinners would respond to God on that occasion any differently than they have already responded in life on earth. There is no reason to the think they would. . . . Someone like Herod . . . would only hate God all the more on the last day because he would see more grace in God to hate" [*WGM*, 171].)

Inclusivists answer the question of whether this form of a postmortem encounter diminishes the urgency of missions. "This question would have greater force if we knew who the premessianic believers were, whereas in actual fact they are mixed in with populations that need to hear the gospel" (*WGM*, 172). The answer of course is that we do not know who the believers will be. It is interesting that similar "missionary urgency" questions are asked of those who hold to election as saving.[45] And their answer is similar, too. Because we do not know the identity of the elect, who are mixed with the non-elect, the question is mute. Postmortem opportunity for salvation is the anthropological parallel of divine election in the question of the identity of the saved and the urgency of missions. Neither answer addresses the question. Regardless of arguments to the contrary, postmortem salvific opportunities or a saving election view theologically and practically dampen the urgency for missions. Actually, why should God patiently wait for more to repent (*WGM*, 176; cf. 2 Peter 3:9) if they could do it in the next life? Is it only because they are not born? But then there would be no question at all.

One may not widen the condition of salvation (its terms or time) for many to be saved. However, it is possible to widen the numbers to be saved, without widening the condition of salvation (i.e., for those who cannot meet the condition—infants who die and the mentally incompetent). Inclusivists want both. They desire to widen the salvific condition and numbers of saved on earth without widening the condition in eternity. Of course, if the widened salvific condition raised the numbers of the saved already, there is no postmortem need in eternity.[46]

We may ask another question of the inclusivists here. If death is not a momentous boundary, why confirm the decision of active Christ rejecters at death and not the more passive decision of rejection by others? For instance, what about the category of the religious man who has heard the gospel and rejects Christ, but still continues in meeting the internal and external conditions of the faith-principle? Does he need to trust Christ in this life or the next? Why should he be given another chance if he met the criteria of the faith-principle but consciously rejected Christ? Why not confirm his lack of earthly desire or decision for Christ at death, as God would do to the more heinous unbeliever? (Pinnock mentions Herod in this category [*WGM*, 170].). If he is given an opportunity for salvation, then those who knowingly reject Christ should also have a second chance at eternity. At least in this case (and a growing number fit this bill) even the conscious non-acceptance or rejection of Christ does not disqualify a person from eternal life. Under this kind of framework there would be two kinds of "believers" in addition to Christians. Those who unknowingly reject Christ and meet the faith-principle; and those who knowingly reject Christ and meet the faith-principle.

How Important Are Christian Missions? The wider-hope view's lessening of motivation for Christian missions is often the primary objection raised against the view. Is missions an absolute necessity if people's need to hear the gospel is not? Pinnock's suspicion against those who raise the objection is "that we have narrowed the motivation for missions down to this one thing: deliverance from wrath."[47] But "coming at missions from the perspective of the kingdom explains why everybody without exception needs to hear the Good News. . . . God wants everybody to be part of the kingdom movement" (*WGM*, 178). "Like the early Christians, we go in obedience to the Lord's command, with a concern for the glory of God, and in the power of the Holy Spirit" (ibid.).

What inclusivists include and exclude as motivation for missions is revealing. The obedience to the Great Commission and the surge of the kingdom are lofty motives for missions. However, they are but partial in the total structure of missions motivation in the Bible, especially when orienting such Christian activity to this life alone. I would reiterate that judgment consequences of not believing in Jesus extend to the afterlife (cf. John 3:16; 5:24, 29).[48] Inclusivists overlook a whole biblical theology of postmortem punishment for those who may not be grossly wicked (Matt. 5:29–30; 18:9) and for the actively wicked (Matt. 23:33; cf. Mark 9:43, 45, 47). When everyone is said to be without excuse (Rom. 1:20), it is not only without excuse "of" knowledge of God, but without excuse "from" the judgment of God. (cf. Rom. 2:5, 16, "day of wrath"). Even though all men have light (rational, moral, existential light, John 1:9), they still have to come into the salvific light (John 3:19–21). So, prior to belief in Christ, even men who may not love darkness (cf. John 3:19) are still condemned because they have not believed in Him (John 3:18). Now, the more grave the sin, the more the condemnation (Luke 12:47–48). However, the entire argument of inclusivism against the traditional view of hell is based on sins of commission, that is especially of the active and gross kind (cf. sins of omissions, Luke 12:47; James 4:17) and negates the universal rendering of all being under sin (Rom. 3:9) and personally coming short of the glory of God (Rom. 3:23).[49]

Pinnock prefers 2 Thessalonians 1:8 to refer to those "who knowingly and willingly are God's enemies and want to remain so. . . . Those who will suffer neither obey the Gospel nor any other form of revelation they have been given" (*WGM*, 175). These are

surmised to be the culpably arrogant, rather than inculpably ignorant. However, in addition to clearly proving the "eternal" duration
of the destruction of the wicked (cf. Isa. 33:14; 66:24; Matt. 3:12;
13:42–43; 18:8; 25:41; Rev. 14:10–11; 20:10, 15)[50], 2 Thessalonians
1:8 has a contribution to make to our immediate issue. There are
two possible interpretations of the verse. The entire range of the
unsaved may be specified here—from those who are "ignorant"
("those who do not know God," cf. Eph. 2:12; Gal. 4:8; 1 Thess.
4:5) to those who are "arrogant" ("do not obey the gospel of our
Lord Jesus"). Or to turn the verse toward Pinnock's more unlikely
view, "those who do not 'obey the gospel of our Lord' may be said
to have knowingly rejected Christ." However, the link between
"knowing God" and "not obeying the gospel of Christ" is inescap-
able. That is, one cannot truly know God without obeying the gospel of Christ. The first interpretation emphasizes eternal hell for all
those who are ignorant of God, and the second says a person is
ignorant of God if he does not obey the gospel of Christ. So, either
rendering proves difficult for the inclusivist position.

Motivations for missions involves the eternal destiny of the
unevangelized whether they were ignorant of the gospel or disobe-
dient to it. Proclamation compounds culpability (John 15:22; cf.
9:41), and it would be actually better for Pinnock's believers not to
hear the gospel and have a postmortem chance to go to heaven
rather than having believed in God and rejected the gospel. The
latter seems to be the case of most sincere non-Christians who are
immersed in their own religions.

We do not disagree that the gospel has major resources and
implications for the present life, but it seems unjust for God to have
kept full-strength salvation from pre-Messianic believers of Old and
New Testaments just because some human disobeyed Christ's
commands for a surge of God's kingdom. Actually, if people can
be saved without Christ (Melchizedek, Job), why is it not possible
that people can have fullness of life without Christ? Why cannot a
just God give fullness of life, for this life, apart from Christ, too?

Also, once a condition for damnation (or salvation) is placed
the inclusivist thesis fails. The implicit assumption is that a person
must know about Christ in order to be justly condemned (cf. *NON*,
39). Why cannot we also assume that a person must know about
God (for Christian inclusivists, the God of Jesus Christ) in order to
be justly condemned? Again, large masses of humanity hailing

from non-theistic frameworks do not worship this theistic God (and a Christian theistic God) either. Is it just to condemn them as inclusivists would have to espouse? Their view turns out be just as restrictive as the more traditional one.

My argument is if Jesus spoke and warned about hell (e.g., Matt. 10:28 and verses in the previous sections of this chapter), it should be a primary motivation for missions.[51] Second Corinthians 5:11 counts missionary zeal as arising from the fear of the Lord. In this passage, the primary reference of the "fear of the Lord" is the Christian's appearance at the judgment seat of Christ (v. 10; cf. 1 Peter 1:17). But because the principle that "each one receives what is due for things done while in the body" (2 Cor. 5:10) is an unchanging universal (Matt. 16:27; Rom. 2:6; 1 Peter 1:17), Paul may have been motivated by the prospect of a fearful non-Christian future as well. This is best illustrated in the two missionary sermons of Paul to those in non-Christian religions. Acts 10:42 and 17:31 mention the judgment motif to non-Christians, who were candidates for the inclusivist pre-Messianic believer status. This of course undermines the inclusivist position.

I conclude by pointing out the difficulty in embracing Pinnock's summarizing call to missions, "Premessianic believers, along with many others, need to be challenged to seek God, because they have not yet done so" (*WGM*, 179). But his whole book has already argued that pre-Messianic believers have already sought and found God in their own ways.

Notes

1. Hans Kung, Roman Catholic theologian and a principal writer of the global ethic, reported by Michael Hirsley, "Religion Parliament Sees More Discord than Unity," *Chicago Tribune,* 5 September 1993, sec. 3, p. 1.

2. Laurie Goodstein, "'Declaration of a Global Ethic' Signed at Religious Parliament: Paper Seeks to Define Common Set of Values for World in Agony," *Washington Post,* 3 September 1993, A3.

3. Peter Steinfels, "More Diversity Than Harmony: Road to Religious Understanding is Filled with Pitfalls," *New York Times,* 7 September 1993, A11.

4. The distinction follows W. C. Smith, *The Meaning and End of Religion* (New York: Macmillan, 1962); and Paul Tillich's definition of religion in *Christianity and the Encounter of the World Religions* (New York: Columbia Univ., 1963). Both writers follow an existential and privatized description of true religion over and against doctrinal content and propositional affirmations.

5. Harold A. Netland, *Dissonant Voices: Religious Pluralism and The Question of Truth* (Grand Rapids: Eerdmans, 1991), 35.

6. Netland, 127. We have already noticed Pinnock's incipient or emergent pluralism. Netland writes that pluralists "have confused the question of truth with that of the believer's response to the truth" (131).

7. Rev. Palaniswami, a Hindu priest in Hawaii and editor of *Hinduism Today,* not only writes "An Open Letter to Evangelicals," but he provides the first attempt of modern Hinduism to put a Hindu creed on paper (*World Pulse,* 8 February 1991, 2–3).

8. K. Cragg, *The Christ and the Faiths* (Philadelphia: Westminster, 1986), 221.

9. Netland admirably reflects on various aspects of Hick's comprehensive theory of religions and criticizes it as tantamount to reductionism because "each tradition ascribes ultimacy to its own particular conceptions of the religious ultimate" (222).

10. Cf. John J. Collins, ed., "Apocalypse: The Morphology of a Genre," *Semeia* 14 (Missoula, Mont.: Scholars Press, 1979) who concludes that the difference between Johannine and Jewish apocalyptic writings are superficial; and G. E. Ladd, "Apocalyptic and NT Theology," in *Reconciliation and Hope,* ed. Robert Banks, (Grand Rapids: Eerdmans, 1974), 285–96, who sees major differences between these apocalyptic literature.

11. See the fine chapter on "Influences on the Religion of the Hebrews," in R. K. Harrison, *Introduction to the Old Testament* (Grand Rapids: Eerdmans, 1969), 381–95, which disavows the influence of animism, tabu, totemism, ancestor worship, and the methodological approach of Wellhausen, who applied a biological view of origins to biblical criticism, concluding that theistic religion was a latter development in the evolution of religions.

12. Creation and Flood mythologies are compared with the biblical accounts for convergence, divergence, and source, in Keith W. Jeske, "A Comparison of Ancient Creation Myths and the Biblical Account of Creation," Th.M. thesis (Dallas Theological Seminary, 1979); and J. S. Bose, "A Comparison of the Indian Flood Accounts with those of the Ancient Near East and the Old Testament," Th.M. thesis (Dallas Theological Seminary, 1978).

13. A side of Pinnock's bibliology can be discerned in the context of this "borrowing" feature. Because of Israelite failure, "Yahweh is portrayed on occasion as cruel and peevish? What else can be the meaning of the side of God seen in certain texts of the Old Testament (like Ex 4:24)? Does this stem from the human side of Scripture?" (*WGM,* 88).

We do not know what this "human side of Scripture" refers to—its "erroneous" side or its "borrowing" side? It may be the former: "It appears that the Old Testament did not always capture the divine nature with full accuracy" (ibid.). We have attempted to prove that Pinnock's neglect of divine severity was not a full and accurate capture of the divine nature in the Old Testament. Or in the latter case, we have the Old Testament not only borrowing "positive" features, but "negative" features from environmentally influenced human writers. This view is a dilution of the quality of divine revelation in the Christian Scriptures.

14. For example, the prohibition of boiling a kid in its mother's milk, S. Ananda Kumar, "Culture and the Old Testament," in *Down to Earth: Studies in Christianity and Culture*, ed. John R. W. Stott and Robert Coote (Grand Rapids: Eerdmans, 1980), 41.

15. Ananda Kumar, p. 48, notes, "To speak in terms of one of our examples, Genesis 1 is the Word of God for us, not the Babylonian Creation Epic, even though the former may be appreciated best when seen against the background of the latter."

16. Carl E. Braaten, *No Other Gospel!: Christianity Among the World's Religions* (Minneapolis: Fortress, 1992), 97–98.

17. See under *hilaskomai, katallasso,* the *lutrow* word group, *sozo* and *soter,* in Colin Brown, gen. ed., *New International Dictionary of New Testament Theology (DNTT)*. 3 vols. (Grand Rapids: Zondervan, 1975), 3:148–76, 3:189–223. A quick overview may be found in Carl Wilson, "Salvation, Save, Savior," in E. F. Harrison, ed., *Baker's Dictionary of Theology (BDT)* (Grand Rapids: Baker, 1960), 468–70.

18. Pinnock wants the benefit of "God's presence and revelation in other religions" (*WGM*, 106–7) to explain their positive features. However, if he is forced to address their salvific potency and value, I think he would deduce, at least at present, the conclusion proposed in our text.

   Being more positive does not require us to conclude that every religion is a vehicle of salvation or an ordinary way of salvation. . . . Even faith-responses can be made in the context of other religions as in the case of Melchizedek and Jethro (both pagan priests). Their religions seem to have been vehicles of salvation for them. (Ibid., 107)

19. The problem is accentuated in dealing with Christian and Muslim concepts of "Allah." The more abstract the concept (e.g., "God is one"), the more the similarity. The more concrete the concept (e.g., God is disclosed in Jesus Christ or the Quran) the more the conflict. This is why there is still debate as to whether "Allah" should be used in a Christian context at all. For instance, the Indonesian Christian use of "Allah" seems to be more "Christian" than the Middle Eastern Christian use of "Allah." (See the attempt at equation and differentiation by Imad N. Shehadeh, "A Comparison and a Contrast Between the Prologue of John's Gospel and Quranic Surah 5," Th.D. diss., Dallas Theological Seminary, 1990), chaps. 3–5. A philosophical problem in theological discussion on the interreligious subject emerges: "Is there a concept without a context?" I hasten to answer in the negative, at least in the language of religions.

20. *World Pulse*, 27 (24 April 1992): 6–7.

21. Alister E. McGrath, "The Challenge of Pluralism for the Contemporary Christian Church," *Journal of the Evangelical Theological Society (JETS)* 35:3 (September 1992): 361–73, brings out a similar point, "We must therefore be intensely suspicious of the naive assumption that 'religions' is a well-defined category that can be sharply and surgically distinguished from 'culture' as a whole" (369).

22. His argument is unacceptable inasmuch as Pinnock uses it to prove his optimism toward the religions from the point. Max Black clarifies the "begging the question" fallacy: "It should be noted that circular arguments are not necessarily invalid; the ground for condemning such argu-

ments is their fruitlessness as proofs" (cf. Max Black, *Critical Thinking* [Englewood Cliffs, N. J.: Prentice-Hall, 1952], 237).

23. Steinfels, *New York Times*, A11.

24. See Black, *Critical Thinking*, 234.

25. *WGM*, 104. "Job, Enoch and Noah all seem to have responded to them" [i.e., general revelation and prevenient grace] (*WGM*, 105).

Pinnock uses Deuteronomy 4:19 to mean, "Yahweh permitted the nations to worship him in ways not proper for Israel to do" (*WGM*, 101). The text does not indicate that the nations were worshiping Yahweh. The nations were at best worshiping the stars. Yahweh had allotted and apportioned that worship, but did not approve of it. The nations were not worshiping Him.

26. This, in the face of Sanders's criticism that evangelicals see conversion as primarily informational. Instead, "The true purpose for missions is 'stimulating the hearers to action,' not just imparting new information" (*NON*, 267).

Thinking through this matter forces a contradiction in Pinnock and Sanders. If "the principal problem is will, not ignorance" (*NON*, 267), then the question does not arise in the first place, for the opportunity not to know about Christ was the problem they put up. However, if the problem is in the human will, then special and more revelation itself will not solve the problem of just condemnation. We shall soon see that Pinnock prefers to view human departure from God as more intellectual than moral.

27. An adaptation from A. J. Hoover, *Don't You Believe it!* (Chicago: Moody, 1982), 94, on the difference between necessary and sufficient causation.

28. There is much written on the subjects of ecumenical and evangelical notions of dialogue. For an introduction there is chapter 13, "Trends in the Theology of Religions: Types of Contemporary Dialogue," in J. Verkuyl, *Contemporary Missiology* (Grand Rapids: Eerdmans, 1978); and A. F. Glasser, "A Paradigm Shift? Evangelicals and Interreligious Dialogue," *Missiology* 9 (December 1981): 393–408.

29. William C. Placher, *Unapologetic Theology: A Christian Voice in a Pluralistic Conversation* (Louisville: Westminster/John Knox, 1989), chap. 5. Placher discusses J. Habermas and J. Rawls as promoting this notion and takes John Hick to task for ideological imperialism hiding in pluralistic vocabulary. On the "eschatological verification" notion in Hick, Placher appropriately notes: "I would argue that a Christian not only expects a different destination but also claims to see a different pattern in the road itself" (p. 136, n. 11).

30. See my remarks on an adequate philosophy of history in "Elements of a Biblical Philosophy of History," *Bibliotheca Sacra* 138 (April-June 1981): 108–18.

31. See John Hick, *Evil and the God of Love* (New York: Harper & Row, 1966), chap. 17.

32. *WGM*, 146. In addition to the link with Hick is also the link with Karl Rahner. Even though Pinnock does not agree with Rahner's theory of lawful religion, where religions are the main sphere of God's activity (79), and dismisses Rahner's position "as naive speculation" (91), there are several

stated and unstated connections couched in more conservative terminology. Pinnock's two axioms are from Rahner's "Christianity and the Non-Christian Religions," in *Theological Investigations* 5 (London: Darton, Longman and Todd, 1966), 115–34. Pinnock's subscription to Vatican II positions and the emphasis on the Logos doctrine (36, n. 28) are large evidences of this connection. While Rahner suggested the category of the "anonymous Christian," Pinnock could suggest the "anonymous believer" along with the "anonymous Christ" emerging from a Logos Christology: "the Logos is not confined to one segment of human history or one piece of world geography" (77).

33. Cf. the contrast to those who are implicated with universalism from a corporate elective angle, there are those who hold to a corporate emphasis and a restrictivist position. See Robert Shank, *Elect in the Son: A Study of the Doctrine of Election* (Springfield, Mo.: Westcott, 1970).

34. Pinnock himself documents, translates, and finds support for the theological conversation between the major positions in two books he has edited, *The Grace of God and The Will of Man* (Grand Rapids: Zondervan, Academie Books, 1989) and his earlier *Grace Unlimited* (Minneapolis: Bethany Fellowship, 1975).

   An examination of common truths between Arminianism and Calvinism is found in Edward Fudge, "How Wide is God's Mercy?," *Christianity Today,* 27 April 1992, 30–33.

   A theological comment on an issue that Sanders brings to us is needed. Using the language of medieval theology, inclusivists see Jesus as the "final cause" of salvation, whereas those who insist that knowledge of Christ is necessary for salvation view Jesus as the "efficient cause." "Inclusivists believe the efficient cause to be an act of faith in accord with the knowledge of God that the individual possesses" (*NON*, 265). Or, Pinnock assumes the efficient causality of faith in making this statement, "If God did not accept people whose religious faith was deficient, who among us could stand before him" (*WGM*, 101).

   All people's religious faith is deficient. Nobody gets accepted on the *basis* of their religious faith. The position I am laying out does not hold to faith as an Arminian efficient cause nor to election as a Calvinist efficient cause of salvation. Instead, "faith in Christ" is the *instrumental* cause of salvation. I think this position preserves the necessity of faith (election does not save nor is it the only saving instrumentality, contra Calvinism) without making it a "work" (contra Arminianism).

35. *WGM*, 159. From Stuart C. Hackett, *The Reconstruction of the Christian Revelation Claim* (Grand Rapids: Baker, 1984), 244.

36. See L. S. Chafer on the accomplishments of the cross, *Systematic Theology* (Dallas: Dallas Seminary, 1948), 3: chaps. 11ff.

37. Unfortunately, we see parity between Sanders's position and his own description of universalism or its implications:

   Universalists urge Christians to move from a Christ-centered faith that excludes other people to a God-centered faith that includes others by claiming that all religions are acceptable. (*NON*, 115–16)

   Sanders now explains his own position:

> Inclusivism [is] the contention that salvation is presently universally accessible even if people are never evangelized, that if they make a faith commitment to God they will be saved by the atonement of Jesus even though they have never heard about that grace. (5)

There is parity between the beyond/non-Christ, "God-centered faith" positions of inclusivists and universalists. And again,

> Inclusivists argue that the salvation God so magnanimously gives is, and has been, available in every age and culture and spot on the globe apart from any specific knowledge of God's historical activity in Israel and in his son Jesus. (216)

This statement too is reminiscent of the universalistic move from a "Christ-centered faith that excludes other people." And again,

> Inclusivists concede that in an ontological sense their salvation ultimately depended on the atonement of Jesus, since no one is saved apart from the redemptive work of Christ. . . . But inclusivists hold that while the source of salvific water is the same for all people, it comes to various people through different channels. (226)

This assertion also is a move from a Christ-centered faith that excludes other peoples, to a God-centered faith that includes all people by claiming that different salvific channels are acceptable.

38. Pinnock's statement that the "corporate emphasis contrasts rather sharply with the popular evangelical view which focuses on the much narrower issue of verbal assent to the gospel—or the decision for Christ" (*WGM*, 151) generates a pertinent comment. According to Matthew 7, verbal assent to the gospel as seen in naming the name of Christ is not enough for salvation. Evangelicals have not held verbal assent to be the sole condition for salvation. The "decision for Christ" is more than verbal or even intellectual assent.

39. Contrary to Pinnock, unevangelized infants are not saved because of 2 Corinthians 5:19 (a problem passage for the limited atonement position).

Also, Warfield is not "a universalist when it comes to babies" (*WGM*, 167). Pinnock needs some precision here. Warfield is a universalist when it comes to babies who die, if that term can be used for this theory at all. Or, we may call him a universalist when it comes to the elect!

In the salvation scheme of many Calvinists, election is God's only saving instrument. Truly, restrictivists who hold a strict view of election could be wider in their salvific theories for "any one whom God has elected, is guaranteed salvation." In this election scheme, there is no logical need for the cross or the response of faith. Indeed, this position could have the widest possible hope, since election becomes the continuing thread of redemption regardless of time, location, or dispensation. These proponents would be reticent to follow through with the logic, but they can consistently hold the ensuing conclusion. In the same way that Job or Melchizedek were chosen and saved, others could be, even though they have not had Christ's salvation explained to them. And this is based on the ontology of the cross. Thus a strong doctrine of election and Pinnock's position may be similar in certain respects. I shall speak more to this issue in the next chapter.

40. See Robert Lightner, *Heaven for Those Who Can't Believe* (Schaumburg, Ill.: Regular Baptist Press, 1977).

41. Notice that the criticisms levied against the divine "middle knowledge" (*WGM*, 160–61; cf. William L. Craig, "Middle Knowledge, A Calvinist-Arminian Rapprochement, in *The Grace of God and The Will of Man*, 141–64) argument does not apply to this position, because this exception is not a hypothetical state of affairs. When it comes to the relationship of babies and the mentally competent to salvation, there are no genuinely unforeseen things. Consequently, God does not judge them on the basis of whether they would have accepted Christ if they had the right facilities and faculties, but excepts them on the basis of being unable to accept salvation, at any point in their lives, whether evangelized or not. Divine foreknowledge concerns genuine freedom (would and would nots) and not genuine ability (could and could nots). Also, Sanders and Pinnock sound alike in their dismissal of the middle knowledge argument, especially in the citation of Jeremiah 3:7 (*WGM*, 161; *NON*, 175). It is interesting to note that when this latter passage is used against the "middle knowledge" position, Pinnock and Sanders seem to be open to God's "thoughts" for Israel's repentance being frustrated (Jer. 3:7), but are not that open to God's "desires" for universal repentance being frustrated (2 Peter 3:9).

42. The exegetical and theological difficulties of the passage make it a weak support for a pillar truth of inclusivism. The passage has spawned reams of material all through church history. A sample bibliography can be had from A. Grillmeier, "Der Gottesohn im Totenreich," in *Mit Ihm Und In Ihm: Christologisch Forshcungen and Perspectiven* (Freiburg: Herder, 1975), 76–174. Also, see William J. Dalton, *Christ's Proclamation to the Spirits* (Rome: Pontifical Biblical Institute, 1965). For a recent proposal, read Wayne Grudem, "He did not Descend into Hell: A Plea for Following Scripture Instead of the Apostles Creed," *Journal of the Evangelical Theological Society* 34 (March 1991): 103–14.

43. Second Corinthians 5:10 does not even give the Christian an excuse for his earthly behavior: "We must all appear before the judgment seat of Christ, that each one may receive what is due him for the things done while in this body, whether good or bad." For the Christian, it is the giving or depriving of reward (cf. 2 Tim. 4:8).

44. Pinnock prefers heaven as an intrinsic rather than an extrinsic reward. The Bible sees heaven as both. Some things that God has prepared for those who love Him are beyond our ability to conceive (1 Cor. 2:9); others are revealed (1 Cor. 2:10) and are commensurate and compatible with earthly disposition and performance (cf. 2 Tim. 4:8; 1 Peter 5:4). However, "heaven offers nothing that a mercenary soul can desire. It is safe to tell the pure in heart that they shall see God, for only the pure in heart want to" (C. S. Lewis, *The Problem of Pain* [New York: Macmillan, 1947], 133).

45. Pinnock hints at this of Augustinian restrictivists, "What motive is there for missions if one believes that it has been decided from eternity who will and who will not be saved" (*WGM*, 177).

46. In this regard, Donald Bloesch would take the wider-hope view to task, and in this way he is more consistent. He holds to faith in Christ as the only means to salvation but provides for an opportunity in the afterlife (*Essentials of Evangelical Theology* [San Francisco: Harper & Row, 1978], 1:244; recognized by Sanders, *NON*, 265).

47. *WGM*, 177. The comment may be reversed. The wider-hope thesis is built around one major motivation too—delivering people from wrath.

48. On the subject of hell, I again direct the reader to Larry Dixon, *The Other Side of the Good News* (Wheaton, Ill.: Victor Books, Bridgepoint, 1992), for a fine and popular treatment of recent objections to the biblical doctrine. Pinnock's "conditional" view of hell, along with his objections to the traditional view of hell, is best articulated in William Crockett, ed., *Four Views of Hell* (Grand Rapids: Zondervan, 1992).

49. I wish for us to note K. Kantzer's comment in the preface of Crockett and Sigountos, "Is there anything that could have been added to help us as we approach the problems addressed in this volume? Yes, there is. Or so, at least, it seems to me. We need a deep sense of the awfulness of sin" (*Through No Fault of their Own*, 14). Somehow those who write on the topic seem to forget to include this basic issue. "But the awful ugliness and repulsiveness of sin did not seem to me to shine through with a crystal brilliance characteristic of the writings of Moses and Isaiah and Paul and John. Could it be that the church is facing the issue of the lostness of humankind in acute form today because as a people we have lost a biblical sense of the awfulness of sin?" (ibid., 14).

50. The discounting of the eternal duration and conscious nature of hell among North American evangelicals has taken significant dimensions with the coming out of the eminent British evangelical, John R. W. Stott in *Evangelical Essentials* (London: Hodder & Stoughton, 1988). For discussion and critique, see Robert L. Reymond, "Dr. John Stott on Hell," *Presbyterion*, 16:26 (Spring 1990): 41–59; and Alan W. Gomes, "Evangelicals and the Annihilation of Hell, Part Two," *Christian Research Journal* 14 (Summer 1991): 9–13.

51. Just stating a need for missions is not enough. Even universalists see a need for missions. Jacques Ellul, who declares his belief in universalism, "no one will be condemned, but everyone will be judged" still sees a need for missions in *What I Believe* (Grand Rapids: Eerdmans, 1989), 207–9. The issue is if missions is structurally needed within such a system. Pinnock's tension with evangelical doctrine is again seen in this matter: "Clearly it (eschatological wrath) is a factor not to be excluded, though it should not dominate the picture" (*WGM*, 180).

5
EVANGELICAL THEOLOGIES AND GOD'S PARTICULAR TRUTH: IMPLICATIONS OF A THEOLOGY OF DISCONTINUITY

Friends took us out sailing recently. It was my first time; it will probably be my last time as well. I thought one just sat there and enjoyed the ambience. However, it was a demanding activity, and our hosts had a lot of work to do. They may teach me how to sail, they will never teach me why.

In positioning the boat to catch the wind, our sailor kept watching the "Windex" (wind index). Perched on top of the main sail mast, the wind index consists of two marker flags and a roving arrow. The red flags are about 45 degrees apart. The roving arrow shows the direction of the wind. While sailing, the arrow can be anywhere in the wider part of the sphere. The arrow had 315 degrees of freedom. But no part of it was to enter the prohibited 45-degree area. If the arrow remained within the ample parameters, it would mean an advantageous sailing position for the boat. Indeed, at a particular angle, the arrow helped the sailor position the boat for maximum propulsion. If the arrow strayed into the prohibited area, the boat would slow down. Unless the direction of the arrow was corrected, the boat was pretty much dead in the water.

A slightly more technical version of this chapter appeared in *Bibliotheca Sacra* 151, no. 601 (January-March 1994): 85–108.

The Scriptures are the "Windex" for the Christian's theological creations and re-creations. Between its covers, there is ample freedom for theological thought, creativity, movement, and application. Indeed, at a certain slant of the theological arrow, there is maximum advantage. Once the theological arrow moves outside the boundaries of Scriptures, the journey will slow down. Unless the direction is corrected, a genuinely biblical expedition is pretty much impossible.

We have examined inclusivism as a soteriological option for evangelicalism and found it to have strayed into a prohibited area, outside the guiding flags of Scripture. In this chapter, we shall examine two evangelical theologies of salvation that rove within the boundaries of Scripture. We especially find one theology of salvation to be at an advantageous angle to provide direction in skilfully answering the difficult set of questions posed by inclusivism.

Again the critical question is, "Are the masses of the world condemned to eternal, conscious punishment even though they cannot be faulted for not having heard the gospel of Christ during their earthly life?" The options for a theologically and emotionally satisfying answer are basic and few. If one is not to be ambiguous and tentative, he must either deny or broaden the exclusive condition of salvation that evangelicals have traditionally subscribed to. Denying the exclusive condition of salvation is not an evangelical option at all. The inclusivist answer to the question, though emotionally appealing, is not biblically plausible, theologically sustainable, or evangelically permissible.[1] The theological arrow of inclusivism strays outside the boundaries of Scripture.

Now let us ponder the same critical question from the perspective of a theology of discontinuity, namely, dispensationalism,[2] as a sub-species of present evangelical theologies. Such a need for this approach arises from certain arguments that Pinnock and Sanders put forth in defense of an inclusivist or "wider hope"[3] position. We have already looked at most of their arguments and the force of their conclusions. Here I present critical interaction from the viewpoints of a dispensational theology of discontinuity and shall conclude with the resources of such a theology to answer the question of the fate of the unevangelized. Within this position, the theological arrow gives strong reassurance for a solid, scriptural answer.[4]

As seen in the first chapter, the inclusivist position gains strength from Jews in the Old Testament who were saved without actually confessing Christ.[5] Again, another piece of theological support for inclusivism comes from the "holy pagan" tradition of Melchizedek, Abimelech, and other pre- or non-Jewish examples.[6] The conclusion to these opening arguments of inclusivism is clear. People may be saved today without knowledge of Jesus Christ, even as was true for people who were saved before Christ.

> While everyone will grant that it was possible to respond to God the way Job did in premessianic times, not everyone thinks that the possibility still exists. This latter hesitation needs to be confronted. Why would it make any difference if Job were born in A.D. 1900 in outer Mongolia? Why would God not deal with him the same way he dealt with him in the Old Testament? A person who is informationally messianic, whether living in ancient or modern times, is in exactly the same spiritual situation. (*WGM*, 161)

On inclusivist premises, the conclusion seems valid. Of course, the conclusion provides a measure of hope for religious individuals all over the world.

EVANGELICAL RESPONSES
TO THE CRITICAL QUESTION

Evangelicals will rightly interrogate these inclusivist hope premises and spurn the conclusion. The covenant position, with some variations, counters that people before Christ did actually confess Him in an embryonic but developing way. (I am not discussing Lutheran, Methodist, Episcopalian, or Roman Catholic theologies of salvation. Covenant theology is an aspect of most Reformed theologies, but it is not equivalent to all non-dispensationalist theology.) Therefore, people today must actually confess Christ for salvation. The dispensationalist rebuts the inclusivist premise in another way.[7] It is true, they would say, that people were saved without actually confessing Christ, but that does not mean they did not confess anything specific. Every dispensation has a specific and exclusive content to faith. In this dispensation, the actual and concrete confession of Christ is necessary for eternal salvation. In either the covenant or dispensational answer, the inclusivist premises and conclusions are disallowed.

THE CRITICAL QUESTION

This problem is plainly one of interdispensational and inter-testamental relationship, because the components of the time of historical existence and the content of salvation are attached to the question of faith. Or to phrase the critical question differently: *Is it possible to affirm that, in the face of the marked lack of knowledge of Christ in the Old Testament, the quality, reality, and vitality of Old Testament salvation is as valid as New Testament salvation, while at the same time preserving the New Testament necessity of explicit knowledge and trust of Christ for eternal salvation?* If there is an acceptable theological means by which this question can be answered affirmatively, then we can effectively discount the inclusivist conclusion about the epistemological non-necessity of Jesus Christ in the New Testament, while allowing for Old Testament salvation outside of explicit knowledge of Christ.

Covenant Theology and the Critical Question

Covenant theologians question the first part of the critical question. For them, there is materially no difference between the content of faith in the Old and New Testaments. A necessary postulate of their position during Old Testament times is an embryonic knowledge of Christ as the One to come. Many would hold that Old Testament saints knew enough about the Seed of Abraham, the Greater Moses, the Lion of Judah, the Son of David, or the Servant of Isaiah to be saved. Messianic themes, shadows, allusions, prefigurements in typological prophecy, and other connections between the Old and New Testaments are strong testimony to this line of specific knowledge of Christ by the Old Testament believer. For the purposes of this chapter, I shall call this the Christocentric "continuity" position.[8]

Roger Nicole addresses the question of the "heathen" and the uniqueness of Jesus from a covenant perspective. He notes that Abraham (John 8:56), Moses (John 5:46), and the Old Testament prophets (1 Peter 1:10–11) "sensed they were speaking about the salvation to come through the work of Christ."[9] Or as Charles Hodge wrote, "It was not mere faith or trust in God, or simple piety, which was required, but faith in the promised Redeemer, or faith in the promise of redemption through the Messiah."[10] Calvin wrote that "the people of God *before* Christ were 'adopted into the hope of immortality' and had full assurance of their salvation (II.x.2), because of God's grace and because their hope was *in Christ,* 'the Mediator, through whom they were joined to God and were to share in his promises' (II.x.2)."[11]

Inclusivism and the Critical Question

The so-called wider-hope position of inclusivism plays up this marked lack of knowledge of Christ in the Old Testament to deny the second part of the critical question. It follows for inclusivists that explicit knowledge of Christ was and is not necessary for eternal salvation at any time in history. Inasmuch as historical impossibility of a knowledge of Christ during Old Testament times did not prohibit salvation by faith in God, neither is specific knowledge of Christ necessary now. I shall refer to this as the "faith-principle" position. (Pinnock constantly refers to what may be termed a "faith-principle," unrelated to specific, salvific content, as connecting the saved of the Old and the New. See especially *WGM,* 157–63.) Pinnock writes, "In my judgment, the faith principle is the basis of universal accessibility. According to the Bible, people are saved by faith, not by the content of their theology" (*WGM,* 157). Or as Sanders maintains, "Inclusivists do not claim that people are saved by their righteousness; they contend that people like Cornelius are saved because they have the 'habit of faith,' which involves penitence. But inclusivists do claim that it is not necessary to understand the work of Christ in order to be saved" (*NON,* 223).

THE RESPONSES OF A
THEOLOGY OF DISCONTINUITY

Covenant theology, inclusivist theology, and dispensational theology agree on the ontology of salvation. That is, anyone who is saved at any time is saved on or by the atoning work of Jesus Christ. The critical points of difference relate to the epistemology of salvation—the question of whether faith explicitly in Christ is necessary to be saved.

Dispensationalism and Covenant Theology

Dispensationalism questions the significant amount of knowledge that covenant theology requires of all Israelites who were saved in the Old Testament. Ryrie raises the question clear-ly.[12] In covenant theology, "little is said of how much the Israelite understood what those illustrations [of redemption in the Old Testament sacrificial system] represented. The reason for this is very plain—it is very difficult if not impossible to prove that the average Israelite understood the grace of God in Christ"[13] Ross pursues a similar complaint: "The Old Testament shows no evidence of such revelation [that the person and work of Jesus Christ was literally revealed to old Testament believers] and the New Testament wit-nesses against it. . . . It is most improbable that everyone who be-lieved unto salvation consciously believed in the substitutionary death of Jesus Christ, the Son of God."[14]

So, dispensationalism raises major questions about the amount of content of salvific truth that was historically available during the epochs of the Old Testament. Even if one allows certain Old Testa-ment personalities a great degree of Christocentric knowledge by divine revelatory initiatives such as covenant, vision, dreams, and other personal means of normative revelation, the number of per-sons who had access to such extraordinary salvific content is rath-er insignificant—so much so that such revelations cannot be made the norm and source of widespread salvation during the entire Old Testament.[15]

Dispensationalism Considers Inclusivism

Along with covenant theology,[16] dispensationalism questions the inclusivist view of a generic, contentless, salvation-bringing faith-principle in the Old Testament, let alone in the New Testa-ment. Although inclusivists are anxious to use Ryrie's words to emphasize the basis, the requirement, and the object of faith in salvation, they overlook a structural characteristic of a dispensa-tional theology of salvation—the *specific content* that was neces-sary in each dispensation. "It is this last point, of course, which distinguishes dispensationalism from covenant theology."[17] I has-ten to add that it is this last point that distinguishes dispensationa-lism from the inclusivist view, too. As Ross puts it, "Ultimately the content of saving faith in any age must be God *and* his revelation concerning participation in his covenant (what we call salvation). Believers were ultimately taking God at his *word* when they re-sponded to *the truth* in their situations. But as revelation contin-ued, the content of faith grew" (italics added; Ross, 172).

Old Testament saints (Abrahamite, pre- and non-Abrahamite saints) did not display a habit of a contentless faith. Their faith-content was specified, required, and therefore exclusive. That is, an epistemology of exclusivity is not just a New Testament phenomenon introduced in Jesus Christ. When one takes the Old Testament's epistemology of exclusivity and adds the fuller, clarified New Testament insistence on explicit, conscious knowledge and belief in Christ as the means of receiving eternal salvation, the inclusivist, wider-hope view becomes inadmissible.

To summarize dispensational differences with the covenant (continuity) position, it assumes a great amount of Christological knowledge by the typical Israelite. It argues from the few to the many. Just because Job, Abraham, Moses, and David knew much about the Coming One does not lead to the conclusion that all who were saved knew much about the Coming One.

The dispensationalist problem with the inclusivist (faith-principle) position is similar to its problem with the continuity position. The inclusivist opinion has to assume a great amount of faith in the right object on the part of many unmentioned non-Abrahamites/Israelites based on the example of a few non-Abrahamites/Israelites who are named to salvation. This position also argues from the few to the many. Just because Abel, Melchizedek, Noah, Jethro, and Naaman were saved does not lead to the conclusion that most of those outside contact with and knowledge of YHWH were also saved.

Both the continuity and faith-principle theologies commit the fallacy of the general rule. They argue for a general rule from a small sample. That is, in the covenant scheme, a few cases of specific Christocentric knowledge become a case for the widespread and necessary availability of specific Christocentric knowledge. Or in an inclusivist scheme, every case of non-Israelite salvation becomes a case for the general availability of salvation without an exclusive content condition. And as far as biblical information (sheer numbers?) goes, most pre- and non-Abrahamites/Israelites were judged and destroyed in the Flood—we could also include the later intent of "Canaanite" destruction. If one needs to argue for a general rule, it must not be based on too small a sample. Against inclusivism, the general rule actually yields widespread judgement rather than salvation. As we have seen earlier, there are several "neglected factors" and "disconfirmatory instances" to both these theologies of salvation. Let me summarize the three positions with a diagram.

Theology of Salvation	Continuity	Faith-Principle	Discontinuity
Object of Faith	God	God	God
Requirement	Faith	Faith	Faith
Basis of Salvation	Cross	Cross	Cross
Content of Faith [Old Testament Era]	Specific: Progressive Christocentric	Unspecific: Constant Theocentric	Specific: Incremental[18] Epoch-Related
Content of Faith [New Testament Era]	Specific: Christocentric	Unspecific: Theocentric	Specific: Christocentric

Although there are similarities in the argumentation process, there is no connection between the conclusions of covenant theologians and the inclusivist view. One major dividing line between the two theologies is the application of the generalizations. There are actual evidences and examples of Old Testament saints who had heavier and higher amounts of insight into the Promised Redeemer (for example, Abraham, Moses, David, etc.). Therefore, the conclusions of covenant theology are plausible. Our question to them only relates to whether this sampling is representative and proportionate to the entire Old Testament population of saints. On the other hand, the inclusivist view has not established one biblical instance of salvation by "the direction of heart rather than the content of theology." ("The issue God cares about is the direction of the heart, not the content of theology," WGM, 158.) There is no biblical evidence of an abstract faith-principle toward God, without specific theological truth, bringing salvation. Consequently, Pinnock and Sanders must make an enormous inductive leap. This leap is exegetically unsound and logically questionable.[19]

The thesis of the rest of this book is as follows. A dispensational reading of the biblical history of salvation provides adequate theological resources to (1) preserve Old Testament salvation outside explicit knowledge of Christ, and (2) insist that explicit knowledge of Christ is an exclusive, universal condition for salvation in the present epoch. If the historical and hermeneutical distinctions between the dispensations[20] are eliminated, a broadened condition for salvation could become evangelically viable.

SOME IMPLICATIONS FROM DISPENSATIONAL DISCONTINUITY

From the preceding comments, historical location and epistemological content in the historical flow of salvation become critically important. Theologies of salvation relate historical location and epistemology in different ways. For universalists, neither time nor content is critical to salvation. For inclusivists, a time-related epistemology is inconsequential. For covenant theologians, a Christocentric epistemology provides unity to the progress of redemption, with historical location seemingly less important.

However, for dispensationalists,[21] historical location is integrated with epistemological content. One of the distinctives of dispensationalism may well hover on this point that the specific content of saving faith defines, demarcates, and distinguishes a dispensation. Such a distinctive is important in relation to the inclusivist question. That is, it is possible for people to be saved without explicit knowledge of Christ before Christ came, but not after He came. In this way, we preserve the truth and the adequacy of Old Testament revelation for salvation, while emphasizing that in this age "a personal relationship with God is mediated *exclusively* through the Son."[22]

This "integrative" dispensational view of the time and content of salvation provides several theological resources for evangelical interaction against inclusivism. We shall look at dispensational resources against the wider-hope view soteriologically, ecclesiologically, and eschatologically.

Soteriological Implications

First, in dispensationalism the details of Old Testament salvation are given equitable weight in the tight linkage between historical location and salvation epistemology. Pre-Israelites, non-Israelites, and nominal Israelites could be saved as they rightly related to God by exercising faith in the specifically, divinely revealed content for that epoch. During Old Testament times salvation was possible even if Christ was not explicitly known by most Old Testament saints. Embryonic or mature salvific knowledge of Christ is attributed to divine revelatory initiatives that dispensed insight into the movement of the Messianic promise to significant patriarchal and prophetic human carriers (Abel, Noah, Abraham, Moses, David, Isaiah, Jeremiah, Daniel, etc.; cf. Heb. 11). And yet, these patriarchs and prophets did not necessarily understand many dimensions of what they uttered (cf. 1 Peter 1:10–11). Also, after the inception of the race and the nation, non-Israelites who are named as saved came into contact with Israelites and had to acknowledge the God of Israel (e.g., queen of Sheba and Solomon, Naaman and Elisha, Nebuchadnezzar and Daniel).

Second, in dispensationalism, the details of New Testament salvation are also given equitable weight in the tight linkage between historical location and salvation epistemology. The pre-Christian or non-Christian and the nominal Christian can be saved as they rightly relate to God by exercising faith in the specifically and divinely revealed content for this epoch (John 3:16; Acts 4:12; 16:31; etc.). Even now, divine revelatory initiatives may dispense insight into the arrival of the Messianic promise, but any such recipient (e.g., a Hindu or Muslim seeker) must still relate to Jesus Christ (cf., Cornelius, Acts 10:43). That is, divine revelatory initiatives are not salvific. A person must explicitly believe in the salvific content of this dispensation, namely, on the Lord Jesus Christ as his or her only God and Savior.

Third, while affirming the unchanging and unchangeable ontology of salvation (e.g., divine election, the atonement, etc.) integrative dispensationalism carries the requirement of epistemological exclusivity throughout the epochs of history. Therefore, a quantitatively lesser amount of Messianic knowledge in the Old Testament is not deemed to be qualitatively inferior.[23]

For instance, dispensationalism would not permit a glossing over of the pre-Israelite period, as many are prone to do. Sanders (and Porphyry, the neo-Platonist from Tyre who assailed early Christianity) discusses a legitimate concern.

Porphyry was aware that some Christians attempted to meet his objection by claiming that people before Christ were saved by faith in the Christ to come. Pagans, before Christ, it was argued, were saved if they turned to the Jewish faith, which taught about the Christ who was to come. To this Porphyry said:

> Let it not be said that provision had been made for the human race by the old Jewish law. It was only after a long time that the Jewish law appeared and flourished within the narrow limits of Syria. . . . It gradually crept onwards to the coasts of Italy; but this was not earlier than the end of the reign of Gaius. . . . What, then, became of the souls of men in Rome and Latium who lived before the time of the Caesars, and were destitute of the grace of Christ, because He had not then come?[24]

Sanders and Porphyry force us into a pre- (and/or non-) Israelite dispensation with some validity. Dispensationalists answer from a time-content integration stance that before the Jews appeared, God had other divinely revealed, specific content for salvation. Once any such content appeared on the earth, people everywhere had to relate properly to the God who was communicated *in* the content. Pre-Israelite salvation was just as real and vital as salvation proffered at any other time in human history. In this way, dispensationalism also protects from the inference that a pre-Israelite period was the archetypal dispensation for the paradigm of salvation—a necessary assumption of the inclusivist view.

Fourth, dispensationalism insists that the temporal, geographical, and epistemological extent of salvation are coterminous aspects. This view is possible because the amount of Messianic (salvific?) knowledge given to Abraham or David did not have to extend to all Old Testament saved people regardless of place, time, or content of revelation. We relate this point to Pinnock's argument in the case of Abimelech's salvation (Gen. 20). "He [Abimelech] was in fact another pagan who had a right relation with God outside the boundaries of Israel's covenant" (*WGM*, 26). From this Pinnock deduces that the boundaries of Israel's covenant are similar to the boundaries of Jesus' salvation. Inasmuch as Abimelech was outside Israel, Pinnock reasons, those who do not know of Jesus also can be saved.

Even if one grants (with questions) Abimelech's dream of divine accountability, protests of a clean conscience, compensatory generosity, and his healing as synonyms of personal salvation, we make the following comments. The coterminous view of the temporal, geographical, and epistemological extent of salvation demands that specific content was for the human race at a given time, regardless of the accidents and circumstance of one's birth place. The "holy pagan" passages actually prove that Yahwistic salvation was for the whole world (as in the Abimelech-Abraham interchange). This salvation was available before Israel and continued through the duration of Israel to be available to non-Israelites. And this is so with the New Testament. The temporal, geographical, and epistemological are coterminous. (Although Pinnock mentions Abimelech's tryst with Abraham [Gen. 20], he does not mention a highly similar event with another pagan, Pharaoh [Gen. 12:10–20]. The implications for inclusivism from the earlier episode are not promising.)

For the sake of discussion, let us say (erroneously) that YHWH's salvation was only for Israel, and that people in the Old Testament could be saved outside the boundaries of Israel. This still does not indicate that people can be saved outside Jesus today. Whatever one takes Israel's covenant geography to be, Jesus' salvation is clearly universal (as proved by inclusivist use of the universal texts). Dispensational discontinuity allows for Old Testament salvation to relate only to Israel and yet to have the New Testament relate to the whole world. This too is a point in favor of the discontinuity position in a theology of biblical salvation history.

The coterminous aspect of the discussion repeats an earlier charge made against Pinnock's assumption here, "How can we deny, based on this material, that God works outside *so-called* salvation history?" (*WGM*, 27). Just because God has worked (past tense) outside so-called salvation history, does not mean that He always works outside this "history." Further, for God to work outside salvation history makes salvation history extend beyond its own boundaries. Pinnock has to posit a salvation history *within* salvation history (*Heilsgeschicte im Heilsgeschicte*), in which case the narrow *Heilsgeschicte* (salvation history) becomes vacuous and unnecessary. All that can be said from the Old Testament is that God work*ed* in a particular manner. The discontinuity of the extent and recipients of the content of bibical salvation can be confidently affirmed in a dispensational reading of salvation history. Otherwise in our desire for a generic continuity of the extent and recipients of Old Testament salvation, the inclusivist case may seem preferable.

Ecclesiological[25] Implications

This section examines a few key issues from the perspective of a dispensational ecclesiology in relation to inclusivist propositions.

Believers and Christians. A division between two kinds of saved people is required by the inclusivist view. As cited earlier, Sanders distinguishes between "believers" and "Christians" (*NON*, 224–32. "Inclusivists contend that all Christians are believers but not all believers are Christians" [ibid., 225].). Believers "can be defined as all those who are saved because they have faith in God" (ibid., 224–25). A Christian, of course, is "a believer who knows about and participates in the work of Jesus Christ" (ibid., 225).

Pinnock distinguishes between pre-Messianic believers and Messianic believers—in other words, between two kinds of "Christians" (*WGM*, 105. "Responding positively to premessianic revelation can make them [premessianic believers] right with God, but it cannot make them messianic believers" [ibid.].). Both groups are considered "saved." Pre-Messianic believers presently need Christ and missions for "full strength" salvation in this life: "Unevangelized believers need a clearer revelation of God's love and forgiveness, and the assurance that goes with love and forgiveness."[26]

I have searched for Pinnock's and Sanders's views about the composition of the universal church and have failed to surface any precise comments on the subject. Because they write about the mission of the church, one may infer that they view the whole church as being composed of Christians or Messianic believers who participate in the mission of bringing Christ to the nations, which would include "unevangelized believers" who have not heard of Christ. But whether or not unevangelized believers and pre-Messianic believers are part of the church is not easily recognizable in their writings.

Inclusivism leads to two awkward theological options concerning the composition of the church. The first option, along with evangelicals, is to include only true Christians in the church. But Pinnock has two categories of the saved in relationship to the church—the saved who are in the church and the saved who are not in the church. If inclusivists include only Christians or Messianic believers in the church, they will have to make an additional distinction among the saved—the saved who belong to the church (and therefore are aware of it), and the saved who do not belong to the church (and therefore are unaware of it). Though Pinnock distances himself from Rahner (*WGM*, 79, 91), the latter category implies or sounds like a Rahnerian "Anonymous Christian" view. We could call it an "Anonymous Church" or "Anonymous Believer" view. That is, we do not know they are Christians (Rahner) or in the church (Pinnock), and "saved non-Christians" do not know it either.

Inclusivism's second option on church composition is to make both believers (pre-Messianic) and Messianic Christians as part of the church, though Christians still have to evangelize believers. Here, strangely, we have those who have not believed in Christ as part of the church. That believers already in the church need to be evangelized not only sounds outlandish, but it also reduces mission to the mere task of "conscientization"—announcing and making a certain category of people aware of what is already true about them. This view interjects a distinctly nonevangelical overtone into missions.[27]

A hint about the composition of the church may be found in the following statement, "A forward look characterizes the church age, and central to it is the ingathering of the Gentiles. . . . The central thrust of this present age is the ingathering of the Gentiles through the mission entrusted to us" (*WGM*, 117). Whether these Gentiles include believers is not known, though those who carry the mission are Christians. It seems as though "the church age" here comprises all present believers (Messianic and pre-Messianic) in a universal entity, the church, parts of which are identifiable (Messianic believers) and parts of which are unidentifiable but authentic (pre-Messianic believers). Only self-conscious Christians would belong to what is identifiable as the church and would then carry on the mission of the church.

I bring up this point under ecclesiology (rather than soteriology) because of dispensational insistence that the church is composed of the saved in this age *and* is administratively discontinuous with Israel. One of the essential (not just institutional) differences between the church and Israel involves the means and constituents of those who make up the church and Israel. Even though Israel and the church may be constitutionally and functionally analogous, how one becomes a constituent of each is different. Everyone physically born within the sociopolitical orbit of Israel was a bonafide, ethnic Israelite. But not all ethnic Israelites, Abrahamites of the flesh, were believers, that is, Abrahamites of the promise. To receive salvation, ethnic (children of the flesh) Israelites still had to express personal belief. "Faith found expression in the OT in two predominant ways: obedience to the Law, and worship through sacrifices."[28] In Israel, there were the saved and unsaved. It was possible for the unsaved to be in Israel, though authentic Israelites were not just ethnically so. These were also children of the promise.

Evangelicals hold that it is not possible for the unsaved to belong spiritually in the church. People have to believe personally in Christ to be born into the spiritual orbit of the church. Unlike Israel, the church has no distinction between those who are spiritually related to it and those who are not. That is, in the church, there are no levels of ethnic meaning or tiers of belonging. Consequently, if Israel and the church are continuous or essentially the same, we not only run into soterio-ecclesiological problems, but we also face a major enigma that caters to the inclusivist view. Inclusivists could argue that just as more than authentic Israelites were in Israel, so more than authentic Christians are in the church. Dispensational discontinuity disallows the plausibility of the inclusivist view of tiers of the saved. Only the saved (in the traditional, evangelical sense of that term) belong in the church. They are self-consciously the church with missional responsibilities to the world.

Simultaneous Dispensationalism. One of the powerful arguments for inclusivism in view of the accessibility problem is the presence of so-called simultaneous or concurrent dispensationalism. In this approach, as the name suggests, more than one dispensation runs concurrently. Charles Kraft "distinguishes between the chronological position of those who have never heard and their position with respect to revelational information."[29] This group is chronologically A.D. and informationally B.C. In short, this variety of the unevangelized is in the New Testament dispensation in reference to time and in the Old Testament dispensation in reference to the content of salvation.

This issue may be addressed in several ways. Dispensationalists again point out that Old Testament saints, in spite of their lack of knowledge of Christ, did have divinely revealed, specific content (which demarcates the dispensations, especially between the Old Testament and the New Testament) to believe. If Old Testament believers did not have anything definite to believe, Kraft's point could be acceptable. People today are not in an Old Testament dispensation in terms of specific content. The two eras relate only in terms of lack, that is, in terms of ignorance people may have of Jesus Christ. I again point out that what the religious masses in the populous regions of the world (e.g., China and India) believe today does not even remotely correspond to what Abraham and Melchizedek believed as the divinely revealed specifics of their day.[30] People today, like the unsaved of the Old Testament, and unlike the saved of the Old Testament, indisputably affirm other spiritual doctrines and systems of salvation.

Thus Kraft makes an erroneous cross-dispensational link based on "shared ignorance" between the Old Testament and New Testament. He confuses the content-specifics of the Old Testament, which were believed by saved people like Melchizedek and Naaman (in spite of their ignorance of Christ), with the lack of specifics of Jesus Christ among chronologically A.D. people. People outside Jesus Christ today do not maintain neutral or blank religious minds. Although I acknowledge the information deficiency problem about Christ, I do not acknowledge such a deficiency or ignorance about God. Romans 1 notes that all people know God (v. 21) and the ordinance of God in terms of moral accountability (v. 32).

Too, the Bible points to a "moral" problem among all the unsaved. Their problems in relation to salvation are twofold. They not only are ignorant about Christ, but they are guilty of suppressing truth and committing rebellious actions. In this respect, a continuous, cross-dispensational link exists between the "unsaved" of both Old and New Testaments—both are guilty. The cross-dispensational link is not between the non-Israelites who were saved in the Old Testament and non-Israelites in the New Testament era who are not saved. People in the latter group affirm adverse beliefs that are not the divinely revealed salvation content for this era.

The concept of specific salvation content for a period of time, which affects all humans in that time period, is contrary to the inclusivist "faith-principle" paradigm. This approach seeks a common denominator for salvific content (faith-principle) in the various ages. Once this common, abstract content of salvation is identified, it is given a generic status as the condition of salvation throughout. Inclusivists next attempt to find suitable candidates in any given dispensation to fit this generic condition. However, a newly defined specific for salvation (e.g., belief in Christ) thwarts their efforts.[31] So they posit concurrent dispensations to accommodate pre-Messianic believers, who have merely a generic, abstract understanding of salvation, and Messianic Christians, who have a specific, concrete salvation understanding.

It is here that I tap dispensationalism's philosophy of history regarding the progress of revelation and the giving of the biblical covenants. Its philosophy of history does not allow for simultaneous and concurrent epochs in this or any dispensation. Salvific content is intensively found in divinely revealed specifics. Salvific reach is extensively given temporally and geographically. Intensive content and extensive reach correlate to distinguish the dispensations. History is viewed in a purposeful, linear movement, with all-encompassing "wholes" of time. In this way, any period of salvific revelation in the Bible applies to the entirety of the human race for that time. This view is proposed on a definite temporal *and* comprehensive geographical extent to the revealed content of salvation in history. Repeatedly, specific revelatory events have global dimensions, as witnessed in Adam (global effect of the Fall, Gen. 3); Noah (the global flood and covenant, Gen. 6–8)); Abraham (global promise, Gen. 12); Israel (global orientation, Ex. 19:6; Deut. 4:6–8; Ps. 67, Isa. 60–66); the Cross (global implication, John 3:16; 1 John 2:2); the church (global influence, Matt. 28); the millennium (global reign, Ps. 2; Rev. 20:1–6); and eternity (global "summing up" and new creation, 1 Cor. 15:27–28; Rev. 21–22). Can dispensations be running concurrently now? Theologically this cannot be so, because such a view diminishes the comprehensive, epochal, and global radicalness of the cross and the corresponding uniqueness of the church in God's program.

For this dispensation, the cross is of global significance. This significance has to be more than merely ontological if it relates to all the inhabited earth. Otherwise, the cross might as well have happened just in the realm of the ideal, in an eternal form in God's mind. Simultaneous dispensationalism diminishes the historical radicalness of the cross by taking away its epistemological radicalness and thereby undermining its comprehensive global claim and coverage. To evangelicals, the importance of the cross stems from an ontology (God's perspective) and epistemology (man's perspective) of salvation.

Also in this philosophy of history, but not particular to it, the church is of comprehensive global significance. There is an internationality to the disciple-making mandate (Matt. 28:19). Unfortunately, the church may cultivate an ingrownness as Israel did in confusing elective responsibility with selfish privilege. But in dispensationalism the church by nature and composition portrays a *new* universality that is discontinuous with Israel. It insists that, to a large measure, the church was unforeseen in the Old Testament. Although Gentilic salvation is highly evident in the Old Testament, the equality and heirship of Jews and Gentiles in a corporate body was the mystery that was revealed to the apostles and prophets. So the church is not a limited, nationally constituted institution. By nature it is new, and by composition it is multi-ethnic. If the church is not a new entity with global (space) and epochal (time) significance as the body of Christ, then a simultaneous dispensationalism of the present age could possibly have validity. However, the nonnationalistic, indiscriminate, interracial composition of Christ's body does not allow the premise or promise of simultaneous dispensationalism. The fundamental event of the cross and the composition of the church extend throughout the world in this age. To provide a different content of faith for human salvation in the church age is to regulate post-cross salvation by a pre-cross model and to suggest pre-Pentecost descriptions for a post-Pentecost entity (the church).

So a solid dispensationalist philosophy of history, with its linear movement of time and incremental view of revelation, provides an exhaustive theological resource against the weaknesses of concurrent dispensationalism. It invalidates a "chronologically A.D. and informationally B.C." division as an alternate model for salvation opportunity. Such an ineffectual division is acknowledged by Kraft himself: "The discontinuity from our perspective is in fact that chronologically A.D. people *could* know whereas B.C. people could not know" (*Christianity in Culture*, 255; italics in the original). Certainly this kind of person is not quite unique. Everyone in this dispensation, until he comes to know Christ, fits into the classification of chronologically A.D. and informationally B.C. Consequently, this category of the unevangelized is not unique. (Pinnock desires to show that "many varieties of unevangelized will attain salvation" [WGM, 168]. If by "varieties of the unevangelized," he means varieties of unsaved, then there are only two in relation to life and death. There are only those who have eternal life and those who are already perishing [John 3:16, 17; 2 Cor. 2:15].) Now a post-Christ dispensational location cannot be changed. The pre-Christ ignorance can be corrected in this post-Christ dispensation. Such a correction was not historically possible on a wide scale in a pre-Christ dispensation.

Eschatological Implications

Perhaps, dispensationalism is most popularly known for its eschatological thought. The rise of eschatology as a proper division of biblical and systematic theology may in some way be related to dispensationalists' emphasis on a future for ethnic Israel on the earth. From this futurist orientation of dispensational premillennialism some implications can be brought to bear against an inclusivist interpretation of salvation that sees it as primarily this-worldly and has reduced the criteria for salvific truth.

This-Worldly Salvation. The Old Testament prospect of salvation was spiritual, immediate, and this-worldly. Ross (in J. Feinberg, 178) regards the profile of Old Testament salvation as deliverance from enemies, rest in the land, and unbroken fellowship with God. Though Pinnock does not use it, he could gain a certain Old Testament advantage because he to wants to see the New Testament benefits of salvation as spiritual, immediate, and this-worldly. Of course to make the Old Testament understandings and expectations of salvation parallel to New Testament salvific benefits, some adjustments would be needed. Sociopolitical deliverance from enemies and literal rest in a geographically defined land would have to be adjusted to refer to sin, demons, heaven, and so on.

Dispensational premillennialism, with its futuristic emphasis, enables the prospects of Old Testament salvation to be taken in a plain, originally understood sense. And the discontinuity system does not consent to New Testament salvation as beneficial only in a spiritual, immediate, this-worldly sense. The Old Testament audience, while finding spiritual salvation on earth along with short-term deliverance from enemies, will still see the eschatological realization of geographical hope. But New Testament salvation promises an eternal, ultimate, and other-worldly salvation. It refuses to give eternity second place to an earthly millennium, though the saved from both groupings will enjoy the benefits of an earthly resolution of history *and* an eternal consummation of all things under Christ in a permanent conjoining of identities and destinies. Dispensational eschatology vetoes any simultaneous grading of salvific benefits in the past, present, or future. It does not permit differentiation between a "full-strength," this-worldly, eternally assured salvation for Messianic Christians and a diluted, this-worldly, unassured eternal salvation to pre-Messianic believers. Instead, Old Testament pre-Messianic believers had a vital, full-strength relationship with God and will benefit from an earthly fulfillment of their original understanding and expectations. Such a futurist eschatology preserves the validity of Old Testament prospects of this-worldly salvation without allowing it to subsume New Testament salvation under the Old Testament paradigm.

Criterion for Truth. One of the difficulties in the inclusivist view is ascertaining a criterion for salvific truth that can be applied to non-Christian religions today. Having seen the Bible as providing a generic principle for salvation (e.g., faith commitment to God), but not providing the specifics for salvation (content for explicit trust), inclusivists face the question of how to evaluate truth components in non-Christian religions. A lack of biblical criteria to manage and designate the explicitness of salvific truth allows Pinnock to see Buddhism being in touch with God in its own way (*WGM*, 100; cited earlier), and Muslims and Jews worshiping the same God as Christians (*WGM*, 97; cited earlier). Most evangelicals find these suggestions unacceptable because non-Christian religions do not measure up to the standard of the Scriptures[32] with reference to the condition and possibility for eternal salvation. We now ask if dispensationalism provides an additional resource, from an eschatological standpoint, to discount inclusivism and provide a present criterion for truth.

Dispensationalists look forward to an eschatological time when all believers will participate in the millennial kingdom of Jesus Christ as the final earthly dispensation. This kingdom will be brought about by divine intervention and without human agency. It will also be present in earthly and historical experience. This *historical,* eschatological scenario disallows Pinnock's (and Hicks's) notion of alleviating present decisions about absolute truth by aspiring to the eschatological verification of truth.[33] Their eschatological notion is useless as a truth criterion in and for the present. But truth and falsity cannot be resolved by a nonhistorical, eschatological maneuver, if they cannot be resolved in the historical past or present. The guarantee of eschatological resolution is based on the premise of historical verification. If eschatology could be relegated to a nonhistorical future, then the verifiable claim between the future and the past becomes dim and the historical connection between past, present, and future is severed. When the historical connection is cut, the criterion for truth becomes some nonhistorical ideal rather than a verifiable, historical event that discriminates between truth and error.[34]

In Jesus' incarnation the eschatological King and kingdom were historically present (the *auto-basileia* feature). Whether the kingdom departed from the earth when the King departed from the earth is a matter of discussion between dispensationalists. All dispensationalists are agreed that Jesus the King and the reality of His kingdom were integrally related during the incarnation; that there is a present heavenly seating of Christ at the right hand of God the Father; and that there is a coming earthly reign of Christ. The first area of agreement—Christ as *auto-basileia*—furnishes the critical, historical criterion of truth for the exclusivity of Christ and the evaluation of salvific truth in other religions. This historical reality of past, present, and future follows a dispensational premillennial interpretation. Further, the tight link between the future, earthly, historical absolute of the kingdom, made certain by its relationship to the past, earthly, historical, absolute of King Jesus supplies the critical evaluative and valuative criterion for world religions. The King cannot be divorced from His kingdom. The King has come visibly in history and geography, but the kingdom has not yet come visibly in history and geography. Therefore, the King provides the criteria by which anyone may be included in His kingdom. We do not have to resolve this truth eschatologically. Christians do not have to wait for a teleological (Troeltsch) or eschatological (Hick, Pinnock) verification of this exclusive epistemology of Jesus Christ.

CONCLUSION

The inclusivist view is a "live" and crucial issue for modern evangelical exchange. Dispensationalism stands in the evangelical tradition as a resource for a New Testament epistemology of exclusivity against the inclusivist view. In connection with historical location and salvific epistemology, I review the contours of the inclusivist argument[26] with appropriate comments from an integrative, dispensational viewpoint.

"Pre-Christ people have been saved without explicit knowledge of Christ." However, not having "explicit knowledge of Christ" is only part of the equation of salvation content. Dispensationalism insists that pre-Christ believers did have explicit, concrete content to believe, in their temporal location in the history of salvation. There was divinely revealed, specific content of which there had to be explicit knowledge in order to receive salvation.

"People, then, can be saved without explicit knowledge of Christ." Dispensationalism questions the defensibleness of this salvation principle. Is this "principle" legitimately drawn from the historical fact and narrative of the Old Testament and applicable across history? Inclusivists illicitly disregard the content of salvation at any given time, but arbitrarily give universal status to that time period that yields their principle. They jump from half the fact (what Old Testament believers did and could not have) to an across-the-board application of a method of salvation. It is proper to conclude that people have been saved without knowledge of Christ. But it is improper to conclude from it that anyone anywhere can and will be saved in the same way. Dispensationalism insists on the critical time factor and does not permit usage of an archetypal "faith-principle" that claims that people can and will be saved without knowledge of Christ in this time in human history.

"There are many post-Christ people without explicit knowledge of Christ now." There is no dispute of this fact.

"Therefore these too can be saved without explicit knowledge of Christ as were their pre-Christ counterparts." This conclusion is inadmissible. Pre-Christian times, like post-Christian times, had divinely revealed specifics for salvation. The legitimate, universal principle is that there are divinely revealed specifics of salvation for all humans regardless of time and location of birth. In this dispensation it is explicit knowledge of Christ. Indeed, post-Christian circumstance of birth is not any more or less advantageous for the unevangelized, since pre-Christian times had divinely revealed specifics for salvation as well. On a related note, the history and geography of birth are not necessarily commendable to

the present population of the world. They provide some advantages to the hearing of the gospel, but not necessarily in accepting it. There are other factors in the sequence of salvation than merely information.

Dispensationalism severely questions the premises and constricts the conclusions of the inclusivist, wider-hope argument. It is able to preserve continuity of faith toward God in both the Old and New Testaments while preserving the specificity of the Old Testament and New Testament content of faith. In answer to Pinnock's earlier question, "Why would it make any difference if Job were born in A.D. 1900 in outer Mongolia?", I answer, "It would not, unless one draws upon the definite resources of a discontinuity construct of the history and theology of salvation."

Notes

1. This, in spite of Pinnock's and Sanders's protestations to the contrary. Again, Pinnock claims to be an "orthodox theologian" (*WGM*, 40) and Sanders lists his "agreement with traditional evangelical theology" (*NON*, 32). They do agree that "the exegetical evidence is not plentiful," but certainly hold that "the theological argument is strong" for some of their positions (*WGM*, 172).

2. "Dispensationalism" has often been damned to pitiful existence through caricature. Two recent efforts at counteracting such misrepresentation show the genius, tensions, and change within the movement. John S. Feinberg, ed., *Continuity and Discontinuity: Perspectives on the Relationship Between the Old and New Testaments* (Westchester, Ill.: Crossway, 1988); and Craig A. Blaising and Darrell L. Bock, eds., *Dispensationalism, Israel, and the Church* (Grand Rapids: Zondervan, 1992).

   As this chapter proceeds, my "minimalist" dispensationalist convictions (affirming an administrative discontinuity between Israel and the church as well as Christ's future earthly kingdom) from a non-North American, implicational, missiological perspective will emerge.

3. I wonder why Sanders does not use the phrase "wider hope" as synonymous with or including "inclusivism." He sees both as outside restrictivism (i.e., a traditional Calvinistic, "limited atonement," even double predestinarian view) and universalism (see *NON*, vii–xi). Presumably, inclusivism is to furnish the widest (non-universalistic) hope of all the wider-hope views.

   There are many evangelicals who are not restrictivists in the traditional Calvinistic sense but still insist "that there is no hope whatsoever for salvation apart from their [unevangelized] hearing the message about the person and work of Christ and exercising faith in Christ before they die" (ibid., 37). These evangelicals are theologically wider than five-point Calvinism (for instance, they subscribe to "unlimited atonement") but are narrower than an inclusivist, wider-hope view.

4. Because there is no monolithic dispensational *system*, there are perspectives and emphases. Blaising and Block identify some of these dispensational emphases, though they do not agree with the concept of sine qua non distinctives of dispensationalism; see Blaising and Bock, 379.

5. "Another class of people saved without professing Christ were the Jews who lived before Jesus was born. . . . The Old Testament describes a large number of believing Israelites who trusted in God, though the Messiah had not yet come to them. Yet they exercised saving faith, as did Abraham, and experienced forgiveness, as did David. Their theological knowledge was deficient, measured by New Testament standards, and their understanding of God was limited because they had not encountered Jesus, in whom alone one sees the Father. Nonetheless, they knew God and belonged to the great cloud of witnesses who encourage us (Heb. 12:1). Without actually confessing Jesus Christ, they were saved by his work of redemption" (*WGM*, 163).

   Actually, the examples of Abraham and David are the easy ones to deal with. As a result of God's covenants (Gen. 12 and 17 and 2 Sam. 7; Ps. 16:9–11; John 8:56) these two had possession of far more theological knowledge and spiritual insight than the more common Israelite. Yet these "giants" were not the only people redeemed in the Old Testament. Pinnock could make his case stronger by appealing to the fact that lesser-known Jewish personages could have been saved without actually confessing Jesus.

6. Pinnock writes: "Abel, Noah, Enoch, Job, Jethro, the queen of Sheba, the centurion, Cornelius—all stand as positive proof that the grace of God touches people all over the world and that faith, without which it is impossible to please God, can and does occur outside as well as inside the formal covenant communities" (*WGM*, 162).

   Sanders also defines the issue for us: "Furthermore, if worshippers of Yahweh such as Cornelius were not saved until they heard about Christ, then what of all the other worshippers of God in the Old Testament, such as Moses and David? Were they all damned to hell?" (*NON*, 65).

7. In highlighting this difference between covenant theology and dispensationalism, I do not care to derail or minimize the attempts at theological rapprochement between these rival perspectives. Both the covenant and dispensational systems are going through development and modification (see Blaising and Bock, and also Vern Poythress, *Understanding Dispensationalists* (Grand Rapids: Zondervan, 1987). Both systems have hermeneutical, theological, and worldview principles that make claims for comprehensiveness and internal consistency. The degree of parity between the two systems as found in recent discussion is intriguing, after decades of theological feuding and sectarianism. In the intramural discussions, larger doctrinal issues and missiological applications, such as the subject of this book, are uncomfortable.

8. Continuity is a self-appellation in covenant theology writings. For example, see Willem VanGemeren, "Systems of Continuity," in J. Feinberg, 37–62: "Reformed Theology is an expression of a *continuity* system" (p. 61). Also see Fred H. Klooster, "The Biblical Method of Salvation: A Case for Continuity," ibid., 131–60.

In contrast to the "Christocentric continuity" of covenant theology, dispensationalism can be said to hold to an "epoch-related discontinuity" when it comes to the content of salvation.

Actually there are entire ranges of continuity and discontinuity in how theologians from both spectrums see salvation in the testaments. I deal with the basic meanings of continuity and discontinuity.

9. Roger Nicole, "One Door and Only One?" *Wherever* 4 (1979): 3. Also cited in *NON*, 38, 43.

10. Charles Hodge, *Systematic Theology* (London: Nelson, 1872), 2:366.

11. Cited by VanGemeren, "Systems of Continuity," 39 (italics in the original). VanGemeren does note, "Though some have questioned whether Calvin was a covenant theologian, no one disputes his position as a theologian with a christological focus" (56).

12. Both Pinnock and Sanders approvingly use dispensationalist Charles Ryrie to affirm the fact of Old Testament salvation without great knowledge of Christ. Pinnock quotes Ryrie twice, (*WGM*, 106, 162), and Sanders cites him once (*NON*, 44) for this manifest criticism of covenant theology. All three citations include Ryrie's well-known answer to the "two ways of salvation" objection to dispensationalism, namely, "The *basis* of salvation in every age is the death of Christ; the *requirement* of salvation in every age is faith; the *object* of faith in every age is God; the *content* of faith changes in the various dispensations" (Charles C. Ryrie, *Dispensationalism Today* [Chicago: Moody, 1965], 123, italics in the original).

13. Ryrie, *Dispensationalism Today,* 122–23. He went on to assert,

> The obvious fallacy in the covenant theologian's solution to the problem is that it is an a priori approach which has yielded artificial results. The assumption is that everything about salvation must be the same; therefore the conscious object of the faith of Old Testament saints must have been Christ. (p. 123)

Even though contemporary dispensationalists have toned down Ryrie's criticisms to acknowledge developments within covenant theology, one may ask if an "essential" feature of a "continuity" theology of salvation has to be negotiated to accommodate development within Reformed theology.

14. Allen P. Ross, "The Biblical Method of Salvation: A Case for Discontinuity," in J. Feinberg, 170. "We cannot grant to the OT believer more understanding than the Scripture indicates he had" (p. 171).

15. In the covenant-dispensational discussion, see Fred Klooster, "The Biblical Method of Salvation: A Case for Continuity," in J. Feinberg, 131–60.

16. See Roger Nicole's article cited above and the "the unity of the covenant of grace" approach to Scripture in covenant theology and Willem A. VanGemeren, *The Progress of Redemption: The Story of Salvation from Creation to the New Jerusalem* (Grand Rapids: Zondervan, 1988). In any case, covenant theology is highly and rightly exclusive. It does not permit a generic, contentless epistemology in the Old Testament, let alone in the New Testament. The New Testament is even more defined or advanced in its exclusivity than the Old Testament, because it points to a Savior who has come.

17. Ryrie, *Dispensationalism Today,* 123. Reformed scholar Bruce Waltke argues this difference in "Evangelical Spirituality: A Biblical Scholar's Perspective," *Journal of the Evangelical Theological Society,* 31:1 (March 1988): 9–24:

    > Evangelicals disagree, however, in their understanding of the object of faith. Dispensationalists contend that OT saints believed the Word of God relative to their dispensation, without specific reference to Jesus Christ. Reformed theologians believe that the elect in all dispensations, have always had Christ as the object of their faith. (12)

18. One may refine the distinction between covenant and dispensational views of progressive revelation. It appears that in covenant theology, there is a progressive unfolding of the core redemptive content—a quantitative issue. (I leave myself open to correction from Reformed theologians on this, or any other, point.) In dispensational theology, there is newness to the additions—qualitative increments through the epochs. In either case, both are agreed that Jesus is the universal and exclusive epistemological issue for this age. When asked for exact definitions, both theologies share similar notions of progressive or incremental revelation.

19. Inclusivism is also not theologically or emotionally that resourceful. The problem of the high numbers of human masses is still not solved. It still has a manner of exclusivity, though not related to Jesus. One simply has to echo Pinnock's problem with Aquinas's theory of the special human messenger: "the theory is not adequate for the size of the problem" (*WGM,* 166); or his problem with Warfield: "it still leaves large numbers eternally lost in absolute terms, even though the overall percentage is lowered" (ibid., 42).

20. The number of dispensations is always a matter of intrigue in any discussion of dispensationalism. Dallas Seminary faculty annually sign a doctrinal statement that highlights only three dispensations—Israel, church, and kingdom—a statement that may be signed by most premillennialists.

    Several covenant theologians also recognize the progressive character of God's redemption in history "emphasizing much more the discontinuities and advances not only between Old Testament and New Testament, but between successive epochs within the Old Testament" (Poythress, 40).

21. Again I refer to "dispensationalism" in the moderate, minimalist sense of a branch of evangelicalism that maintains distinctions between Israel and the church in the administration of God's program in history. May I suggest the following features of the "integrative" relationship between Israel and the church?

    (1) *Ontological unity* of God's kingdom program based on God's eternal nature and unchanging plans.
    (2) *Redemptive continuity* of the saved through history premised on God's unique salvation in Christ Jesus.
    (3) *Administrative discontinuity* in the supervision and execution of the divine program in space-time history, emerging from the consistent use of a valid hermeneutical method.
    (4) *Functional analogy* between the people(s) of God in all ages in their spiritual competence and earthly calling.

All correlations to the inclusivist view in this chapter arise from implications and extrapolations relative to points three and four.

22. Bruce Demarest, in *General Revelation* (Grand Rapids: Zondervan, 1982), voices the phrase in his comments on Matthew 11:27: "Jesus teaches in this text that knowledge of God in the sense of a personal relationship is a gift of the sovereign God mediated exclusively through the Son" (p. 253).

23. This "qualitative inferiority" because of "quantitatively less" knowledge is one of the reasons I argue that the phrase "progressive revelation" be replaced with the more appropriate "incremental revelation." (See again, "Selected Issues in Theoretical Hermeneutics, Part I: Methodological Proposals for Scripture Relevance," *Bibliotheca Sacra* 143 [January-March 1986]: 14–25.)

24. *NON*, p. 52. Pinnock uses Porphyry (from Augustine in a letter to Deogratias; Philip Schaff, ed., *Nicene and Post-Nicene Fathers*, series 1 [1886; reprint, Grand Rapids: Eerdmans, 1974], 1:416) as well:

> If Christ declares himself to be the way of salvation, the grace and truth, and affirms that in him alone, and only to souls believing in him, is the way of return to God, what has become of the men who lived in the many centuries before Christ came? (*WGM*, 149)

Sanders cites Porphyry (ibid., n. 35).

25. The distinction between soteriology and ecclesiology as major segments of systematic theology allows dispensationalism to be separated from the soteriological systems (Calvinism, Moderate Calvinism, Arminianism, etc.). As a hermeneutical principle first, dispensationalism is employed by many soteriological traditions. A personal response to John Gerstner's dismissal of Calvinistic dispensationalism as an oxymoron (*Wrongly Dividing the World of Truth: A Critique of Dispensationalism* [Brentwood, Tenn.: Wolgemuth & Hyatt, 1991]) is that these two systems have distinct, theological "drivers" to their respective structures. Calvinism is soteriologically driven; dispensationalism is ecclesiologically driven. For dispensationalism, the church is an independently valid historical entity even though it is not an ontologically distinct entity. Although I do not hold to the older *parenthetical* (the "after-thought" view) identity to the church in dispensationalism, I also do not hold to a *parasitic* ("footnote") view of the church in God's redemptive plans.

26. Ibid., 178. Sanders quotes J. N. D. Anderson, *Christianity and Comparative Religion* (Downers Grove, Ill.: InterVarsity, 1977), 99, in the same vein:

> Does ignorance disqualify for grace? If so, where in Scripture do we have the exact amount of knowledge required set out? For *assurance*, no doubt, knowledge is required, but for grace it is not so much knowledge as a right attitude towards God that matters. (in *NON*, 225, italics in the original)

27. On an evangelical critique of this and other "Conciliar" views of mission, see Arthur F. Glasser and Donald A. McGavran, *Contemporary Theologies of Missions* (Grand Rapids: Baker, 1983), chaps. 3–5.

28. Ross, "The Biblical Method of Salvation: A Case for Discontinuity," in J. Feinberg, 174.

29. Charles H. Kraft, *Christianity in Culture: A Study in Dynamic Biblical Theologizing in Cross-Cultural Perspective* (Maryknoll, N.Y.: Orbis, 1979), 253.

30. Here we mention a "correspondence" criterion in comparative religious observations: What Old Testament saints confessed does not correspond with what the unreached masses all over the world believe today. We do not question the "how" of the sincere seeker —religious devotion, penitence, and humility (Pinnock's and Sanders's characteristics of faith)— but the "what."

    As discussed in chapter 4, the three great monotheistic religions have vital differences in theistic doctrine (Pinnock recognizes this), even though they can use similar theistic arguments for the existence of God. And, when one compares the "ideas" of God among the populous belief blocks of the world, there are hardly theological parallels to make Kraft's point stick. A comparison of worldviews can be found in Ninian Smart, *World Views: Cross Cultural Exploration of Human Beliefs* (New York: Scribner's, 1983).

31. Here we may ask inclusivists why a latter dispensation cannot provide the archetypal paradigm of salvation? This is covenant theology's alternative and a valid one if its hermeneutical premises and theological principilization are granted. That is, covenant theology classifies Old Testament believers in the chronologically B.C. but informationally (substantially more than in dispensational thinking) A.D. category.

32. I have intentionally not interacted with Pinnock's bibliology because *WGM* does not directly express a bibliology. It does however reveal bibliological positions. While desiring to hold to Scripture as authority (he uses it extensively), Pinnock's theology of religions portrays salvific revelation in the realm of history, outside special, normative revelation. God salvifically reveals Himself, at least indirectly, in ordinary *and* special events of universal history. This salvific revelation is uncovered by the "faith-principle." A question related to this version of "neo-orthodoxy" may be asked. If salvation is possible outside the Bible, why is the Bible treated *as if* it were special at all? These points are raised concerning Pannenberg in Roger E. Olson, Review of *Systematic Theology,* by Wolfhart Pannenberg, translated by Geoffrey W. Bromiley, *Christianity Today,* 22 June 1992, 44.

33. These matters have been mentioned in previous chapters. In the context of the future of religions, Pinnock prefers John Hick's position of some decades ago. "John Hick was right to speak of eschatological verification" (*WGM,* 146). Pinnock also holds that the middle position between relativism and dogmatism in truth-seeking dialogue is epistemologically modest because "truth will be resolved eschatologically. This means that we will never fully resolve the conversation but patiently await the arrival of full knowledge from God" (ibid.).

34. In reading Braaten's recent work, I came across W. Pannenberg's comments on Troeltsch that are relative to the "criteria of truth" issue that has been raised.

    Category of purpose which is so central for Troeltsch does not fit the eschatology of the kingdom of God, because in Jesus' message the coming kingdom is not an extension of human purposes, but comes without any human intervention. . . . Moreover, the influence of the category of final purpose makes Troeltsch give a one-sided emphasis to the kingdom of God as the history of Jesus, an aspect to which he allows only passing significance. Connected with this must also be Troeltsch's inability completely to escape from the difficulties of relativism. Precisely because his idea of the absolute was a final goal in the sense of something totally beyond the present experience of history, present experience in his account necessarily lacks the absolute: its truth lies outside itself. (p. 42)

35. We have seen earlier that Pinnock also appeals to the exceptions that evangelicals across the board make for babies and the mentally incompetent as incentive for including those who have not heard for no fault of their own (*WGM*, 158, 166, 177). The issue of babies and the mentally incompetent is not an exclusive dispensational problem. I do not deal with it here because it is not an argument based on Old Testament salvation patterns. In any case, as pointed out before, just as evangelicals make exceptions for babies, it seems as though the inclusivist also has to make an exception for babies and the mentally incompetent from the "faith-principle."

There may be an additional exception for the faith-principle theology of salvation for religious people who have "heard," do not trust in Christ, and continue with the internal and external evidences of the so-called faith-principle. An increasing number of the unevangelized are coming under this category in this time of technology and missionary presence in global evangelism.

CONCLUSION

Our conversation with the inclusivist position must come to an end. I have declared my agreement with inclusivists at the need for a straightforward position on the critical question. We disagree with theologians who "are not convinced that there is enough information to decide the question" (*NON,* 17). A healthy skepticism about truth and revelation may exhibit submissiveness or snobbishness. It is humble in that it does not want to solve all ultimate questions immediately and conclusively. But it is filled with hubris if indeed it does not want to accept the known and knowable conclusions of biblical revelation. A healthy skepticism about the secret things of the Lord (Deut. 29:29*a*), the judge of all who will do right (Deut. 18:25) exhibits humility. But to diminish "the things revealed (which) belong to us and our sons forever" (Deut. 29:29*b*) displays haughtiness. So, we cannot decide about that which we do not know, but we must steadfastly hold on to conclusions about what we do know.

We disagree with inclusivists about what we do know and conclude. The "things revealed" do not point in the direction of a beyond/outside Jesus salvation for the masses of the world. Biblical revelation and theological arguments on the aspects of salvation do not support the inclusive conclusion. Let me review a few of our theological difficulties with inclusivism.

First, the inclusivist position widens the exclusive condition from the biblical Christ, by one notch, to an idea of God. This move from a specific Christocentric salvation to shared theocentric concepts may appear to be inclusive, except that it carries an intrinsic complication. If this sweeping theocentrism associates with biblical theism, it leaves out masses who do not share the inclusivist's idea of God and often subscribe to contradictory ideas of God among themselves. And if the theocentrism is an abstract conceptualization it ceases to be biblical theism.

Second, in insisting on the "faith-principle," inclusivists have to make exceptions to infants and the mentally incompetent who cannot meet that condition. Consequently, this exception does not carry inclusivist weight against an exclusivist faith-in-Christ position. The exception only illustrates the fact that the faith-in-Christ position has a couple of exceptions too.

Third, inclusivists cannot accept the full meaning of the *universal* salvific will of God for all men to repent. Since they are not strict universalists, they hold to a modified universal salvific will of God. So, the substantive contribution of their first axiomatic postulate, "God's universal will," to the inclusivist position is significantly diluted. Now larger numbers may be expected to be saved under the inclusivists than under the restrictivists. However, even if one person is eternally lost undeservedly (or even deservedly!) the universal salvific will of God is nonuniversal and frustrated to that extent. And we must notice that while the emotional force of the question increases with numbers, the intellectual force of the question is not increased if one or many are lost undeservedly.

Fourth, the specificity of the content of biblical salvation (for example, a biblical theology of the "Name") as the epistemological condition of salvation throughout redemptive history overwhelms the fundamental convictions of inclusivists.

In reading these opposing arguments to inclusivism, we hope that the reader has not only found criticisms but conclusions. I have attempted to construct a dialogue that would produce directions and resources for consistent, comprehensive, coherent, and comforting evangelical solutions to important issues. The constant efforts of theologians at getting evangelicals to open closed doors of interpretation are appreciated. In this case, nevertheless, there is the hazard of jeopardizing the exclusive, unique, sufficient, and necessary self-disclosure of God in Jesus whom all people must believe in order to have eternal life. And this decisive point cannot be negotiated. I am not against change, diversity, or pluralism. These factors are sociological givens, historical imperatives, and pre-evangelistic certainties. While I am for religious plurality (there are many religions in the world) and thus for sociological pluralism,

I am against a redemptive pluralism (there is no diversity of redemptive epistemological options for mankind).

In conclusion, let us open the hard but delicate question again: "Are the masses of the world condemned to endless conscious punishment even though they cannot be faulted in any way for not having heard of the gospel of Christ during their earthly life?"

We could question some plausible assumptions in the question. It may assume that it is a more serious issue that many rather than few are condemned. But maximum experience of joy or pain is on par with the maximum experience of any one person. There are no community multiples of individual experience or a quantitative accumulation of gladness or grief. Endless punishment is as bad as one person is capable of feeling it, and one person in hell is always one person too many. That is why God created hell for the devil and his angels rather than mankind, and desires for all to repent.

The question may also assume that endless conscious punishment is not commensurate with a temporal decision. However, for inclusivists, a postmortem confirmation of rejection will be commensurate with endless conscious punishment (or eternal annihilation) since that decision will be in the nonearthly realm. Not having had the opportunity to hear in *earthly* life gives a person another chance in a future, postmortem experience. Exclusivists and inclusivists agree that earthly life opportunities (or their lack) are important and related to eternal experience. Therefore, the problem of commensurability between earth and eternity is artificially created. It is the same life that continues from earth to eternity. Further, all earthly choices affect eternal experience. Endlessly conscious creatures commit endlessly conscious sin against an endlessly conscious God on the earth resulting in endlessly conscious consequences.

The question may also assume that fault is only appropriately apportioned to those who have had the opportunity to hear and who rejected the gospel in this life. But God can ascribe human fault at many levels. Humans have not properly responded to God's revelation in nature, conscience, history, or reason. Unlike infants and incompetents, they have confirmed their sinfulness by personal acts of rebellion against God and breaking what they know to be right. Certainly, they will not be condemned for what they could not know and thus did not know or do. They will be condemned for what they would not know and thus did not know or do. The points of human guilt deserving eternal separation from God are varied and many. That is, those who have heard and rejected the gospel are doubly at eternal fault. Those who have not heard nor rejected the gospel are singularly at eternal fault.

Early in his book, Sanders writes, "A single statement by our Lord Jesus could have settled the controversy before it began" (*NON*, 18). Evangelicals hold that the Lord Jesus, in fact, did. Only inclusivists do not think it to be conclusive enough. In ending this conversation, let me point the reader to one such place. I refer to John 3:16. If read carefully, each phrase of this "little Gospel" has comprehensive implications for the question that has been addressed from the beginning of this book.

FOR GOD—the God and Father of the Lord Jesus Christ

SO—genuinely and to the highest extent; that is, God could have loved the world less

LOVED—the Christianized word in the best tense possible shows the ontological necessity of God and His love for the salvation sequence

THE WHOLE WORLD—all people, individually and particularly—regardless of time, location, culture, religion, language, etc.,— were the focus of His love

THAT HE GAVE—sacrificial and demonstrative giving

HIS ONE AND ONLY SON—emphasizing the uniqueness of Jesus over all who could become His sons; God gave an irreplaceable Son

THAT WHOSOEVER—an universal invitation to salvation goes out to the whole world that God loved

BELIEVES IN—the responsive principle of faith, accompanied by epistemological necessity

HIM—the one and only Son, referring to the exclusivity of Jesus Christ as the object of faith

SHOULD NOT PERISH—unbelievers in Him are already perishing, not having to do anything to perish eternally (here contrasting "perish" to eternal life)

BUT HAVE—as personal and immediate possession

ETERNAL LIFE—the very life of God beginning now and continuing endlessly, emphasizing the time and arena of decision as this life for the next life.

BIBLIOGRAPHY

Anderson, J. N. D. *Christianity and Comparative Religion.* Downers Grove, Ill.: InterVarsity, 1977.

Bauer, Walter, William F. Arndt, and F. Wilbur Gingrich. *A Greek-English Lexicon of the New Testament and Other Early Christian Literature.* Chicago: Univ. of Chicago, 1957.

Barney, G. Linwood. "Is Decision by Consensus Valid?" *The Alliance Witness,* 20 January 1971, 9–10.

Berhkof, L. *Systematic Theology.* Grand Rapids: Eerdmans, 1939, 1941.

Best, Ernest. *From Text to Sermon: Responsible Use of the New Testament in Preaching.* Edinburgh: T. & T. Clark, 1988 edition.

Black, Max. *Critical Thinking: An Introduction to Logic and Scientific Method.* Englewood Cliffs, N.J.: Prentice-Hall, 1952.

Blaising, Craig A., and Darrell L. Bock, eds. *Dispensationalism, Israel, and the Church.* Grand Rapids: Zondervan, 1992.

Blauw, Johannes. *Missionary Nature of the Church.* New York: McGraw-Hill, 1962.

Bloesch, Donald. *Essentials of Evangelical Theology.* 2 vols. San Francisco: Harper & Row, 1978.

Bose, J. S. "A Comparison of the Indian Flood Accounts with those of the Ancient Near East and the Old Testament." Th.M. thesis, Dallas Theological Seminary, 1978.

Bong Rin Ro and Ruth Eshenaur, eds. *The Bible and Theology in Asian Contexts.* Bangalore: Association of Evangelical Theological Education in India, 1984.

Braaten, Carl E. *No Other Gospel!: Christianity Among the World's Religions.* Minneapolis: Fortress, 1992.

Brown, Colin, gen. ed. *The New International Dictionary of New Testament Theology.* 3 vols. Grand Rapids: Zondervan, 1975.

Brown, David, Robert Jamieson, and A. R. Fausset. *A Commentary: Critical, Experimental and Practical on the Old and New Testaments.* Grand Rapids: Eerdmans, 1978 reprint.

Brown, Francis, S. R. Driver, and Charles A. Briggs. *A Hebrew and English Lexicon of the Old Testament.* Oxford: Clarendon, 1977.

Brown, Harold O. J. Review of *A Wideness in God's Mercy,* by Clark H. Pinnock. *Christianity Today,* 14 September 1992, 40.

Chafer, L. S. *Systematic Theology.* 8 vols. Dallas: Dallas Seminary, 1948.

Collins, John J., ed. "Apocalypse: The Morphology of a Genre." *Semeia* 14. Missoula, Mont.: Scholars Press, 1979.

Cragg, Kenneth. *The Christ and the Faiths.* Philadelphia: Westminster, 1986.

Crockett, William V., and James G. Sigountos, eds. *Through No Fault of Their Own: The Fate of Those Who Have Never Heard.* Grand Rapids: Baker, 1991.

Crockett, William V., ed. *Four Views of Hell.* Grand Rapids: Zondervan, 1992.

Croucher, Rowland. *Recent Trends Among Evangelicals.* Sutherland, Australia: Albatross Books, 1986.

Cutting, G. *Paradigms and Revolutions: Appraisals and Applications of Thomas Kuhn's Philosophy of Science.* Notre Dame-London, 1980.

D'Costa, Gavin. *Theology and Religious Pluralism.* New York: Basil Blackwell, 1986.

Dalton, William J. *Christ's Proclamation to the Spirits.* Rome: Pontifical Biblical Institute, 1965.

Demarest, Bruce. *General Revelation: Historical Views and Contemporary Issues.* Grand Rapids: Zondervan, 1982.

DeRidder, Richard R. *Discipling the Nations.* Grand Rapids: Baker, 1975.

DeSilva, Lynn A. "The Problem of the Self in Buddhism and Christianity." In *What Asian Christians Are Thinking,* edited by Douglas Elwood. Quezon City: New Day, 1978.

Dixon, Larry. *The Other Side of the Good News: Confronting The Contemporary Challenges to Jesus' Teaching on Hell.* Wheaton, Ill.: Victor Books, BridgePoint, 1992.

Elwell, Walter A., ed. *Evangelical Dictionary of Theology.* Grand Rapids: Baker, 1984.

Ellul, Jacques. *What I Believe.* Grand Rapids: Eerdmans, 1989.

Feinberg, John S., and Paul D. Feinberg, eds. *Tradition and Testament: Essays in Honor of Charles Lee Feinberg.* Chicago: Moody, 1981.

Feinberg, John S., ed. *Continuity and Discontinuity: Perspectives on the Relationship Between the Old and New Testaments.* Westchester, Ill.: Crossway, 1988.

Fernando, Ajith. *Crucial Questions About Hell.* Eastbourne, Sussex, England: Kingsway, 1991.

Fudge, Edward. "How Wide is God's Mercy?" *Christianity Today,* 27 April 1992, 30–33.

Gerstner, John. *Wrongly Dividing the World of Truth: A Critique of Dispensationalism.* Brentwood, Tenn.: Wolgemuth & Hyatt, 1991.

Glasser, Arthur F. "A Paradigm Shift? Evangelicals and Interreligious Dialogue." *Missiology* 9 (December 1981): 393–408.

Glasser, Arthur F., and Donald A. McGavran. *Contemporary Theologies of Missions.* Grand Rapids: Baker, 1983.

Gnanakan, Ken. *The Pluralist Predicament.* Bangalore: Theological Book Trust, 1992.

Gomes, Alan W. "Evangelicals and the Annihilation of Hell, Part Two." *Christian Research Journal* 14 (Summer 1991): 9–13.

Grillmeier, A. *Mit Ihm Und In Ihm: Christologisch Forshcungen und Perspectiven.* Freiburg: Herder, 1975.

Grudem, Wayne. "He Did not Descend into Hell: A Plea for Following Scripture instead of the Apostles Creed." *Journal of the Evangelical Theological Society* 34 (March 1991): 103–14.

Guiness, Os, and John Seel, eds. *No God But God: Breaking with the Idols of Our Age.* Chicago: Moody, 1992.

Hackett, Stuart C. *The Reconstruction of the Christian Revelation Claim.* Grand Rapids: Baker, 1984.

Harris, R. Laird, Gleason L. Archer, and Bruce K. Waltke, eds. *Theological Wordbook of the Old Testament.* 2 vols., Chicago: Moody, 1980.

Harrison, Everett F., ed. *Baker's Dictionary of Theology.* Grand Rapids: Baker, 1960.

Harrison, R. K. *Introduction to the Old Testament.* Grand Rapids: Eerdmans, 1969.

Hedlund, Roger E. *Mission to Man in the Bible.* Madras, India: Evangelical Literature Service, 1985.

Hick, John. *Evil and the God of Love.* New York: Harper & Row, 1966.

Hodge, Charles. *Systematic Theology.* London: Nelson, 1872.

Hopper, Jeffery. *Understanding Modern Theology II: Reinterpreting Christian Faith for Changing Worlds.* Philadelphia: Fortress, 1987.

Hoover, A. J. *Don't You Believe It!* Chicago: Moody, 1982.

Jeske, Keith W. "A Comparison of Ancient Creation Myths and the Biblical Account of Creation." Th.M. thesis, Dallas Theological Seminary, 1979.

Kittel, Gerhard, ed. *Theological Dictionary of the New Testament.* Translated by Geoffrey W. Bromiley. 10 vols. Grand Rapids: Eerdmans, 1967.

Kraft, Charles H. *Christianity in Culture: A Study in Dynamic Biblical Theologizing in Cross-Cultural Perspective.* Maryknoll, N. Y.: Orbis, 1979.

Kuhn, Thomas S. *The Structure of Scientific Revolutions.* Chicago: Univ. of Chicago, 1962.

Kung, Hans. *Theology for the Third Millennium: An Ecumenical View.* New York: Doubleday, 1988.

Ladd, G. E. "Apocalyptic and NT Theology." In *Reconciliation and Hope,* edited by Robert Banks. Grand Rapids: Eerdmans, 1974.

Lewis, C. S. *The Abolition of Man.* New York: Macmillan, 1947.

———. *The Problem of Pain.* New York: Macmillan, 1947.

Lightner, Robert. *Heaven for Those Who Can't Believe.* Schaumburg, Ill.: Regular Baptist, 1977.

McGrath, Alister E. "The Challenge of Pluralism for the Contemporary Christian Church." *Journal of the Evangelical Theological Society* 35:3 (September 1992): 361–73.

McKnight, Scot. *A Light Among the Gentiles: Jewish Missionary Activity in the Second Temple Period.* Minneapolis: Fortress, 1991.

Morris, Leon. "Hebrews." *Expositor's Bible Commentary.* Grand Rapids: Zondervan, 1981.

Netland. Harold A. *Dissonant Voices: Religious Pluralism and the Question of Truth.* Grand Rapids: Eerdmans, 1991.

Nicole, Roger. "One Door and Only One?" *Wherever* 4 (1979): 3.

Noll, Mark. "Evangelicals and the Study of the Bible." In *Evangelicalism and Modern America*, edited by George Marsden. Grand Rapids: Eerdmans, 1984, 103–21.

Olson, Roger E. Review of *Systematic Theology*, by Wolfhart Pannenberg. Translated by Geoffrey W. Bromiley. *Christianity Today*, 22 June 1992.

Pailin, David A. *The Anthropological Character of Theology: Conditioning Theological Understanding*. Cambridge, England: Cambridge Univ., 1990.

Palaniswami. "Hinduism." *World Pulse*, 8 February 1991, 2–3.

Pentecost, D. *Things to Come: A Study in Biblical Eschatology*. Grand Rapids: Zondervan, 1964.

Peters, George W. *A Biblical Theology of Missions*. Chicago: Moody, 1972.

Pinnock, Clark H. *Set Forth Your Case: An Examination of Christianity's Credentials*. Chicago: Moody, 1967.

———. *Biblical Revelation: The Foundation of Christian Theology*. Chicago: Moody, 1971.

———., ed. *The Grace of God and the Will of Man: A Case for Arminianism*. Grand Rapids: Zondervan, 1989.

———., ed. *Grace Unlimited*. Minneapolis: Bethany Fellowship, 1975.

———. *Tracking the Maze*. New York: Harper & Row, 1990.

———. "Toward an Evangelical Theology of Religions." *Journal of the Evangelical Theological Society* 33 (1990): 359–68.

———. "The Destruction of the Finally Impenitent." *Criswell Theological Review* 4 (Spring 1990): 243–59.

———. *A Wideness in God's Mercy: The Finality of Jesus Christ in a World of Religions*. Grand Rapids: Zondervan, 1992.

Placher, William. C. *Unapologetic Theology: A Christian Voice in a Pluralistic Conversation*. Louisville: Westminster/John Knox, 1989.

Poliakoff, Michael B. Review of *Believing Today: Jew and Christian in Conversation*, by Leon Klenicki and Richard John Neuhaus. *Journal of the Evangelical Theological Society* 35 (March 1992): 123.

Poythress, Vern. *Understanding Dispensationalists*. Grand Rapids: Zondervan, 1987.

Price, Robert M. "Clark H. Pinnock: Conservative and Contemporary." *Evangelical Quarterly* 88:2 (1988): 157–83.

Rahner, Karl. *Theological Investigations* 5. London: Darton, Longman and Todd, 1966.

Rakestraw, Robert V. "Clark H. Pinnock: A Theological Odyssey." *Christian Scholars Review* 19 (March 1990): 252–70.

Reymond, Robert L. "Dr. John Stott on Hell." *Presbyterion*, 16:26 (Spring 1990): 41–59.

Richard, Ramesh P. "Elements of a Biblical Philosophy of History." *Bibliotheca Sacra* 138 (April-June 1981): 108–18.

———. "Selected Issues in Theoretical Hermeneutics, Part I: Methodological Proposals for Scripture Relevance." *Bibliotheca Sacra* 143 (January-March 1986): 14–25.

———. "Selected Issues in Theoretical Hermeneutics: Part IV: Application Theory in Relation to the Old Testament." *Bibliotheca Sacra* 143 (October-December 1986): 307–10.

Richardson, Alan, and John Bowden, eds. *The Westminster Dictionary of Theology.* Philadelphia: Westminster, 1983.

Richardson, Don. *Eternity in Their Hearts.* Ventura, Calif.: Regal, 1981.

Robertson, A. T. *A Grammar of the Greek New Testament in the Light of Historical Research.* Nashville: Broadman, 1934.

Roenfeldt, Ray C. W. *Clark H. Pinnock on Biblical Authority: An Evolving Position.* Berrien Springs, Mich.: Andrews Univ., 1993.

Ruokanen, Mikka. *The Catholic Doctrine of Non-Christian Religions According to the Second Vatican Council.* Leiden: E. J. Brill, 1992.

Ryrie, Charles C. *Dispensationalism Today.* Chicago: Moody, 1965.

———. *Ryrie Study Bible.* Chicago: Moody, 1978.

Sanders, John. *No Other Name: An Investigation into the Destiny of the Unevangelized.* Grand Rapids: Eerdmans, 1992.

Senior, Donald, and Carroll Stuhlmueller. *The Biblical Foundation for Missions.* Maryknoll, N. Y.: Orbis, 1983.

Shank, Robert. *Elect in the Son: A Study of the Doctrine of Election.* Springfield, Mo.: Westcott, 1970.

Shehadeh, Imad N. "A Comparison and a Contrast Between the Prologue of John's Gospel and Quranic Surah 5." Th.D. diss., Dallas Theological Seminary, 1990.

Smart, Ninian. *World Views: Cross Cultural Exploration of Human Beliefs.* New York: Scribner's, 1983.

Smith, W. C. *The Meaning and End of Religion.* New York: Macmillan, 1962.

Spradley, James P. *The Ethnographic Interview.* New York: Holt, Rinehart and Winston, 1979.

Sproul, R. C. *Objections Answered.* Glendale, Calif.: Regal, 1978.

Stott, John R. W., and Robert Coote. *Down to Earth: Studies in Christianity and Culture.* Grand Rapids: Eerdmans, 1980.

Stott, John R. W. *Evangelical Essentials.* London: Hodder & Stoughton, 1988.

Talmage, E.F., ed. *Disputation and Dialogue: Readings in Jewish/Christian Encounter.* New York: Ktav, 1975.

Tillich, Paul. *Christianity and the Encounter of the World Religions.* New York: Columbia Univ., 1963.

VanGemeren, Willem A. *The Progress of Redemption: The Story of Salvation from Creation to the New Jerusalem.* Grand Rapids: Zondervan, 1988.

Verkuyl, J. *Contemporary Missiology.* Grand Rapids: Eerdmans, 1978.

Waltke, Bruce. "Evangelical Spirituality: A Biblical Scholar's Perspective." *Journal of the Evangelical Theological Society* 31:1 (March 1988): 9–24.

Walvoord, John F., and Roy B. Zuck, eds. *The Bible Knowledge Commentary.* Wheaton, Ill.: Victor Books, 1983.

Walvoord, John F. *Major Bible Prophecies.* Grand Rapids: Zondervan, 1991.

World Pulse, 27 (24 April 1992): 6–7.

Young, Richard Fox. *Resistant Hinduism: Sanskrit Sources on Anti-Christian Apologetics in Early Nineteenth-Century India.* Vienna: Institut fur Indologie der Universitat Wien, 1981.

INDEX OF SUBJECTS AND PERSONS

[Except Clark Pinnock and John Sanders]

Index of Scriptural Books and Texts